FAMOUS
FASHION
DESIGNERS

RALPH LAUREN

FAMOUS
FASHION
DESIGNERS

COCO CHANEL

MARC JACOBS

CALVIN KLEIN

RALPH LAUREN

STELLA McCARTNEY

ISAAC MIZRAHI

VALENTINO

VERSACE

FAMOUS FASHION DESIGNERS

RALPH LAUREN

Joanne Mattern

CHELSEA HOUSE

An Infobase Learning Company

RALPH LAUREN

Copyright © 2011 by Infobase Learning

Chelsea House
An imprint of Infobase Learning
132 West 31st Street
New York NY 10001

Library of Congress Cataloging-in-Publication Data

Mattern, Joanne, 1963–
  Ralph Lauren / by Joanne Mattern.
     p. cm. — (Famous fashion designers)
  Includes bibliographical references and index.
  ISBN 978-1-60413-978-5 (hardcover)
  1. Lauren, Ralph—Juvenile literature. 2. Fashion designers—United States—Biography—Juvenile literature. I. Lauren, Ralph. II. Title.
  TT505.L38M38 2011
  746.9'2092—dc22
  [B]
                                        2010036192

Chelsea House books are available at special discounts when purchased in bulk quantities for businesses, associations, institutions, or sales promotions. Please call our Special Sales Department in New York at (212) 967-8800 or (800) 322-8755.

You can find Chelsea House on the World Wide Web at
http://www.chelseahouse.com

Text design by Lina Farinella
Composition by EJB Publishing Services
Cover design by Alicia Post
Cover printed by Bang Printing, Brainerd, Minn.
Book printed and bound by Bang Printing, Brainerd, Minn.
Date printed: March 2011
Printed in the United States of America

10 9 8 7 6 5 4 3 2 1

Contents

1

Confrontation

It was 1967 and a young man named Ralph Lauren had a big idea. He wanted to design wide ties, a totally different style than what was popular in the United States in the mid-1960s. Lauren had started his own label, called Polo, just a few months earlier. Most ties at that time were dark and narrow, and the style hardly changed from year to year. Lauren's ties were very different. They were shaped like a bottle, wider at the bottom than at the top. Lauren's ties did not come in just solid colors; they had prints and featured bright colors.

Fashion was changing dramatically during the late 1960s. Rock-and-roll music and the hippie culture had added vibrant colors and wild styles to an industry that had always been stiff, bland, and conformist. Lauren carefully watched the fashion trends in England, Italy, and other European countries, and he knew that the new designs he saw there would soon come to the United States and revolutionize what people wore. Lauren wanted to be in the forefront of that revolution.

A SMALL FOLLOWING

Most people did not agree with the young designer, but he did find a few people who understood his vision. Slowly, Lauren was able to convince a few exclusive men's shops to carry his innovative Polo ties. Lauren was very particular about where he sold his ties. In August 1967, Lauren told a reporter, "The romance is where you buy it. The store gives the tie the right or wrong connotations. I want a few good stores, not the commercial market." Lauren knew that by making his product available in only a few select stores, he gave it an air of being special.

Lauren was especially pleased when two high-end stores, Paul Stuart and Meledandri, placed orders for Polo ties. Although neither store ordered a large number of ties, selling his ties to those exclusive outlets gave Lauren prestige, and they made it easier for him to make sales to other stores. It did not take long for Lauren's ties to become a hot item. Sales were still small, however, because only a few stores carried the product.

ELEMENTS OF STYLE

I went to places that had fabrics, piece goods, odds and ends. I went totally in another route than anyone else did. I'd cut up a couch, cut up the fabric just to make the tie. I was so loose in terms of feeling the mood, and I wanted individuality, and I felt there were things that weren't done and I came up with the wide tie and that was my claim to fame.

—*Ralph Lauren in* Genuine Authentic *by Michael Gross*

Starting in menswear, designer Ralph Lauren became famous for his unique, European-inspired clothes. His success allowed him to build a fashion empire that included women's wear, home furnishings, and more.

LAUREN'S BIG DREAM

Lauren's biggest dream was to sell his ties at Bloomingdale's, which was the most influential department store in New York. At the time, Bloomingdale's was the place where the most fashionable people shopped. During the 1960s, wealthy trendsetters flocked to the store every weekend to see and be seen, buying and wearing the latest styles. Lauren knew that if Bloomingdale's stocked his ties, he could achieve his dream of being at the top of the fashion world. "They were there before I was; they were hip, young, exciting," Lauren once said of Bloomingdale's. The only problem was that Bloomingdale's buyers relied on a network of salesmen who had long-standing

To See and Be Seen at Bloomingdale's

In 1860, two brothers named Joseph and Lyman Bloomingdale started carrying ladies hoopskirts in their Ladies' Notion Shop on the Lower East Side of New York. The hoopskirts were a huge fad during the 1860s and helped the brothers' business grow. In 1872, the Bloomingdale brothers broke tradition by opening a store called the East Side Bazaar. At that time, most retailers specialized in selling just one type of garment, but the Bloomingdales sold a wide variety of European fashions, creating the first department store. In 1886, the brothers moved uptown to Fifty-ninth Street and Lexington Avenue, creating a flagship store that eventually grew to cover an entire city block.

Bloomingdale's advertised heavily and also drew shoppers into the store by holding a series of fashion shows and gala events that included music, lighting, and sophisticated sets that rivaled a theatrical production. By the 1960s, Bloomingdale's was the number one store for high fashion, attracting Hollywood celebrities. The queen of England even shopped there in the early 1970s. By using clever marketing campaigns and carrying lines by famous fashion designers such as Ralph Lauren, Perry Ellis, and Norma Kamali, Bloomingdale's became the place where fashionable, wealthy, young trendsetters shopped. Today, with stores in major cities around the United States and even one in the wealthy city of Dubai, United Arab Emirates, Bloomingdale's continues to be a premier department store and a leader in style.

relationships with the store. Lauren was not part of that club, so he had no real chance of getting his product into the store.

In 1967, Lauren finally got the chance he had been waiting for. At that time, Bloomingdale's was actively looking for new talent and was eager to keep pace with other department stores, which were starting to add bold new fashions from European designers. So they were interested when Joe Aezen, a salesman at Rooster Ties and a good friend of Lauren's, began talking about Lauren's products whenever he visited Bloomingdale's on sales calls. He brought samples of Lauren's ties and convinced many of the buyers and managers to wear them. Aezen felt there was no conflict of interest, because Lauren's ties looked nothing like Rooster's more traditional styles and there was little chance the ties would appeal to the same customers. Jack Schultz, who was the divisional merchandise manager, recalled how Aezen would take him and Frank Simon, the men's merchandise manager, to dinner. "All the time he'd be telling us that we had to have those Ralph Lauren ties."

One of the people Aezen talked to was Gary Shafer, who was the buyer for men's fashions at the flagship Bloomingdale's store at Fifty-ninth Street and Lexington Avenue in New York. After hearing Aezen's incessant praise, he decided to do his friend a favor and offer Lauren a spot in the store. Shafer's offer, however, was not quite what Lauren was looking for.

Shafer said that he would buy some of Lauren's ties on two conditions. First, the tie would have to be one-quarter of an inch narrower. Shafer also told Lauren his company name, Polo, could not appear on the ties. Instead, the ties would have to carry the Bloomingdale's label.

Shafer was sure that Lauren would accept his offer. So were all of Lauren's other friends and colleagues. After all, having Polo ties in Bloomingdale's was what Lauren had always wanted, and selling his products at Bloomingdale's would show the world that Lauren was one of the fashion world's top new designers. How could he say no?

In the 1960s, most men wore skinny, solid-colored ties in muted colors. Lauren's large, bottle-shaped ties had bright colors and patterns and made a lasting impression on Bloomingdale's buyers.

A BIG SURPRISE

Lauren did say no. He stunned everyone by refusing Bloomingdale's offer. He told Shafer, "Gary, I'm dying to sell to Bloomingdale's, but I'm closing my bag because I can't take my name off. And I can't make the tie a quarter of an inch narrower." Even though Lauren had always dreamed of selling his ties at Bloomingdale's, he knew that changing the look would make the ties less distinctive and therefore less desirable to buyers. Lauren did not want to sell ties that looked like everyone else's. He wanted to sell what he knew was the future of men's fashion.

Lauren was also too proud to take his company's name off the ties. "I walked out," Lauren said. "Because I believed in who I was." Even though people thought Lauren was crazy for walking away from the deal, he knew that someday Bloomingdale's would come back and ask him to sell his Polo ties in the store—without any changes.

Lauren was right. In time, Bloomingdale's and many other desirable stores would carry Lauren's designs, and he would become one of the most successful and influential fashion designers in history—a designer who always insisted on doing things his way.

2

Growing Up
in New York

R alph Lauren came from very humble beginnings. His childhood experiences were a long way from the glamour and success he achieved as an adult. Still, Lauren's love of fashion played an important role in his life almost from the start.

A SIMPLE LIFE

Ralph Reuban Lifshitz was born on October 14, 1939, in the Bronx, one of the five boroughs of New York City. His parents, Frank and Frieda, had emigrated from Russia to New York with their families when they were teenagers. Frank and Frieda met at an event held by a Jewish social organization and married in 1928. Their first child, a daughter named Thelma, was born in 1930. Then came Leonard, or Lenny, born in 1932; Jerome, or Jerry, born in 1934; and finally Ralph in 1939.

The Lifshitz family lived in a small two-bedroom apartment near a highway called Moshulu Parkway in the Bronx. At the time, the neighborhood was tree lined and surrounded by parks and gardens. Most of the residents were working-class immigrant families who were Jewish, Italian, and Irish. The parents worked as shopkeepers, furriers, garment workers, or in other trades and dreamed of a better life for their children.

Ralph's father, Frank, worked as a house painter. He also painted murals in office buildings around New York City. A family friend, Rabbi Zevulun Charlop, described Frank as "an artist. Everything he did, he did with an artistic touch. He wasn't the ordinary run of house painter. . . . His feet were on the ground and you knew he wanted to soar into the heavens. He was glued to realities. But he wanted to soar. In that way he was altogether different. He had dreams. If Ralph has these qualities now, that's where they come from."

Ralph's mother, Frieda, was more interested in raising her children to be good, observant Jews. Family life was important to her, and religion was the most important element of all. Rabbi Charlop said, "The mother was a strong, forceful figure, very Jewish-minded. Her disappointments in life are that the children didn't necessarily follow in her footsteps in religion. Her profoundest disappointment with Ralph may have been in this area."

Frank and Frieda were careful with their money. Even though Frank earned only fifty to seventy-five dollars a week, the family had everything they needed. "We might have been poor by other people's standards, but in my neighborhood we were comfortable," Ralph said years later. He grew up in a loving home where the children were encouraged to be creative. Sim Storch, a family friend, recalled that "I envied the relaxed atmosphere in their household. The time to spend in artistic exercises was nurtured in that household because of the general quiet and, perhaps, encouragement to be creative." Ralph and his brothers and sister were all good artists. Thelma, who was considered the best artist among the Lifshitz children, later attended New York City's High School of Music and Art.

Originally named Ralph Lifshitz, Lauren grew up in the Bronx in a traditional Jewish family. Lauren *(above center)* wore hand-me-down clothing from his older brothers, Jerry *(right)* and Lenny *(left)*, which drove him to earn money to buy his own clothes.

A LONELY CHILDHOOD

Moshulu Parkway was an exciting and fun place to grow up during the 1940s. The neighborhood was filled with families and children and was very safe. As an adult, Lauren described his childhood in glowing terms. "I would not trade my childhood with anybody. I was very happy. I loved where I grew up. It was fabulous to get out of my house from the age of five, to go down my steps and roller skate through the schoolyard, always somewhere to go."

Neighbors, however, remember young Ralph somewhat differently. They described him as shy and quiet, with a lisp that was later corrected through speech therapy. Ralph spent hours on the front steps, or stoop, of his apartment building, just sitting and thinking. While other children played in a nearby schoolyard, Ralph "sat on the stoop," said a neighbor. "He was always on the stoop. He was a loner. He didn't smile. He was always thinking while the other guys played ball." Ralph was also one of the few boys his age in the neighborhood. Most of the other boys were older and friends with Ralph's brothers. "He was a squirt," said a neighbor boy. "Little Ralphie. That's what everyone called him."

CHILDHOOD HEROES

As Ralph got older, he found more things to do. Like most of the other neighborhood children, he spent almost every Saturday afternoon at the movies, where he could see a movie, several short features, and cartoons for only 10¢. Ralph especially loved cowboy movies and aspired to be John Wayne, who was one of the biggest movie stars of the day. Lauren later wrote: "I thought acting was cool and that I'd have lots of girlfriends. When I'd go to the movies . . . it wasn't just watching John Wayne on the screen—I was the cowboy, I was the man on the horse." He also admired another popular cowboy actor, telling *Vogue* magazine, "I wanted to be Randolph Scott. He was tough, he wasn't a fancy cowboy."

Sports were also a popular pastime in Ralph's neighborhood, especially baseball. Like most boys his age, Lauren idolized Joe

DiMaggio and Mickey Mantle, who played for the New York Yankees. Lauren also liked basketball and would play on his high school team, even though most of the other boys were much taller than he was. "My dream was to be an athlete," he told an interviewer. "I lived sports. That's what I did all day long. My life was playing basketball and stickball. My biggest influences were Joe DiMaggio, Bob Cousy, Sweetwater Clifton. I didn't know what a fashion designer was in high school. It never dawned on me. It was the last thing on my mind."

HIGH SCHOOL DAYS

For most of his childhood, Lauren went to Jewish religious schools, or yeshivas. His mother hoped he would become a rabbi, but Lauren had no interest in following a religious path. He also longed to attend public school. Finally, at the end of his freshman year at yeshiva, he convinced his parents to send him to public school.

Growing Up in New York During the 1950s

New York was an exciting place to be a teenager during the 1950s. Teens gathered on the streets or in parks or schoolyards during the evenings to socialize. They often formed clubs with names like the Earth Angels, Sharks, or Falcons. Other favorite pastimes included "hanging out" at local soda fountains or diners, going to the movies, or attending dances called "sock hops" at local community centers or schools. Garry Marshall, who grew up in the neighborhood and was friends with Ralph Lauren's older brother Lenny, later became a television producer and created the popular show *Happy Days*, which was based on his days growing up in the Moshulu Parkway neighborhood of the Bronx.

In 1954, Lauren began his sophomore year at DeWitt Clinton, an all-boys high school near his home. Right away, Lauren found a way to stand out and attract attention. Although he loved sports, he was not good enough to really excel at being an athlete. Instead, Lauren turned to fashion.

"I was very preppy when most kids didn't know what that was. I wore a lot of oxford shirts and crew neck sweaters. It was unusual in the Bronx at that time because kids were wearing motorcycle jackets."

Steve Bell, who grew up with Lauren and later was one of his business partners, remembered that Lauren had a very different fashion sense from most of the other boys in their neighborhood. "What made him different was that as a kid he'd show up dressed in outrageous stuff, like oversized army ponchos. Or he'd wear these preppy crew neck sweaters in bright colors, and on him they looked great. He had two sharp older brothers, and he saw what they were doing." Indeed, Lauren often benefited by getting hand-me-downs from his older brothers. "I was the baby brother," he recalled. "The clothes went from Lenny to Jerry to me. I guess it was important to have new things, but some of those clothes I really wanted, some of them I couldn't wait to get."

A DIFFERENT WORLD

Lauren was definitely a city boy, but during his teen years he was exposed to a completely different way of life. He went to work at

---

ELEMENTS OF STYLE

I was not a kid who walked around all day in beautiful clothes and pranced in front of a mirror. I was a very natural kid, did all the things everyone did. But I wasn't afraid of taste. I was not afraid of expressing myself, and a lot of kids were.

—*Ralph Lauren in* Genuine Authentic *by Michael Gross*

Lauren's admiration of John Wayne and the cowboy look is reflected in his collections. John Wayne (*above, on horse*), a film icon, starred in many movies, including *The Big Trail*.

Camp Roosevelt, which was a camp for Jewish children in the rural town of Monticello, New York. In those days, Monticello and the surrounding towns were filled with holiday resorts and bungalow colonies where Jewish families could escape the hot, crowded city and enjoy some time out in "the country."

Most of the campers at Camp Roosevelt were from wealthy families, and for the first time, Lauren got a close-up look at a lifestyle that was very different from his own. Lauren liked what he saw. Like many of his friends in the Bronx, Lauren had always dreamed of being successful and having more money than his family, but Camp Roosevelt exposed him to a whole new experience. "It was a very preppy environment," Lauren recalled. "It was much more diversified than what I was used to."

Lauren started working at Camp Roosevelt as a waiter, which he described as being "the lowlife of the camp. The rich kids were the campers and you were working." Despite his lowly position, Lauren took his job seriously and worked hard. By 1956, he had been promoted to counselor, which was a more well-respected and responsible position. Lauren enjoyed his new status. "I'd started nowhere, at the bottom, not knowing anybody, and I worked my way up to being the top counselor. It sounds like nothing now, but at the time, it was very important to me," he later told an interviewer. Camp Roosevelt taught Lauren the importance of hard work and perseverance—lessons that would come in handy as he started his design career.

During his last summer at Camp Roosevelt, sixteen-year-old Ralph decided to change his name from Lifshitz to Lauren. He was tired of being teased because his last name included a profanity. Ralph may have gotten the idea for the name change from his father, who sometimes signed his paintings "Frank Lauren" because he thought "Lauren" sounded more mainstream and Americanized. Ralph's brother Jerry also changed his last name. For Ralph, it was the first step on a journey to a very different life.

3

False Starts

The newly christened Ralph Lauren graduated from DeWitt Clinton High School in 1957. The class yearbook provided a space under each graduate's picture where he or she could list an ambition for the future. Some of the students put "scientist" or "doctor." Lauren listed his ambition as "millionaire." Lauren had a long way to go, however, to achieve his goals.

COLLEGE DAYS

Lauren's family did not have the money to send him to a fancy college, like the boys he had met at Camp Roosevelt. Instead, like his brother Jerry before him, Lauren enrolled at the City College of New York to study business. City College, or CCNY, was located in midtown Manhattan, about an hour away from Lauren's home by subway, and it was a popular, low-cost school for many working-class families in New York.

Although Lauren dreamed of attending a fancy school with a green campus and elegant buildings, instead he found himself attending classes in a midtown office building. Instead of fun and fashion, Lauren was caught in a world of drudgery and boredom. Lauren studied business, but he did not feel like he was learning anything useful that would transform his life. He later described CCNY as "a factory. The whole atmosphere was cold and impersonal."

During his college days, Lauren also worked part-time at a department store called Allied Stores. Lauren, however, was not out in front with his customers. Instead, he worked in a back office. His job was to log in merchandise that was returned to the stores. At first, Lauren enjoyed the job, and he enjoyed the $50 a week he earned for his work. Lauren spent the money on clothes and dates with young women. Lauren soon discovered, however, that many of the salespeople he worked with did not share the same moral standards he did. "A lot of people I met in business did not have integrity. They were not honest," Lauren later said. After a few months, Lauren quit his job to concentrate on school.

Unfortunately, college was not any more rewarding for Lauren. "It was murder," Lauren later described his college days. "I went afternoons and nights and summer school. I was on the trains, it was hot, and I wasn't inspired. My marks were mediocre. I felt school was not what I wanted, so I went back to work." In 1960, he quit college, even though no one was happy about his decision. "I felt, 'Why am I going when everything I'm learning, I'm learning at my work?' I felt I was getting nowhere, so I left. But I was very upset that I did not finish school. It was tough on my family. Everyone went to college, and I was the one that did not make it."

BROOKS BROTHERS

Lauren was determined to find a job, but employment was not easy to come by. At that time, all young men faced being drafted into

When the traditional menswear label Brooks Brothers hired Lauren, the designer finally found himself in the upper-class world he had longed for since he was young. The classic aesthetic would be featured in his clothes, like this double-breasted suit, throughout his career.

the army and having to do months of service for their country. Few companies were willing to hire and train an employee, only to lose him after a few months to the army. Finally, Lauren got lucky.

Lauren enjoyed wearing clothes from Brooks Brothers. The store had been founded in 1818 and was one of the first to carry ready-to-wear clothes, or clothes that were not hand tailored for a specific customer. By the late 1950s, Brooks Brothers was the center of preppy style, and most of its customers came from the high-society, prep-school world Lauren admired so much.

Fortunately for Lauren, his brother Jerry had a friend who was working at Brooks Brothers. Jerry thought that his brother might make a good salesman, and his friend agreed. Lauren got a job selling ties at the store's fashionable Madison Avenue store in Manhattan. He was the store's youngest salesperson and made a decent salary of $65 a week.

Lauren's perfectionism and eye for fashion soon became obvious to everyone around him. "When he finished sorting ties, they looked like soldiers at attention, so beautiful," said Joe Barrato, who worked at Brooks Brothers at the same time Lauren did.

Working at Brooks Brothers was a great learning experience for Lauren. He loved working with the store's upper-class customers and also enjoyed the fancy atmosphere of the store itself. Lauren learned many valuable lessons at Brooks Brothers. He saw that customers expected personal service and that they would pay more to be treated well. Lauren also realized that customers would pay extra for quality materials. His short time at Brooks Brothers had a huge influence on Lauren's career.

ARMY DAYS

Lauren's days at Brooks Brothers did not last long. On December 30, 1960, he was drafted into the U.S. Army. Three months later, Lauren reported for duty at Fort Dix in central New Jersey. There he underwent basic training along with the other new recruits and was assigned a job as a supply clerk.

Not surprisingly, Lauren hated the army. "You have no face, you're not a person, you're a robot." At least Lauren did not mind the clothes, because he had always liked khaki. "I wear khaki. I love army clothes," he later admitted.

Lauren served six months at Fort Dix before returning home to the Bronx. From September 1961 until early 1963, Lauren was on call for the Army Reserve unit in the Bronx and had to be on active duty a few weeks every year. Finally, with his army service completed, Lauren was able to go back to work.

A DYING INDUSTRY

Lauren soon got a job with a glove manufacturer named Meyers Make. At first, Lauren worked in the office, mailing packages of gloves to customers. He had to go through the salesmen's order books and check the orders and where they were being shipped, then stamp and mail the packages. The work was not very interesting, and Lauren had other ideas for his future. He asked his boss, Jerome Fox, to let him become a salesman. Fox admired Lauren's attitude and liked the way he dressed, so he sent him out to try to sell the company's gloves to department-store buyers around the city. Lauren did not have much experience, but he learned as he worked and was always eager and enthusiastic.

Lauren also soaked up information from the other salesmen, who had been on the job for a lot longer than he had. "Basically, I was selling women's gloves that buttoned up to the elbow," Lauren remembered later in his career. "Then I'd sit in on the sales meetings, with some real old-timers, and I'd learn. It was interesting."

Gloves, however, were a dying industry and a victim of the changing fashion trends of the time, which were becoming much less formal than they had been in the past. Also, Lauren was not interested in a career in gloves. "It was obvious that he wasn't cut out for what he was doing," said Frank Arnold, who worked at Meyers Make with Lauren. "You could see his thoughts were elsewhere. He was really interested in men's wear in general, in fashion."

Meyers Make soon went out of business, but shortly before the company folded, Lauren found another job. Once again, he was working for a glove manufacturer, this time for a company called Daniel Hays. He got the job through a friend named Ed Brandau, who had worked with Lauren at Brooks Brothers. Brandau managed the Daniel Hays Company's New York showroom and was happy to have Lauren on board. Like Frank Arnold, however, Brandau could tell that Lauren was not really cut out for the glove industry. "He had a tendency to be a dreamer," Brandau said. "He wasn't really . . . well, how interested in gloves could you be? He was always dreaming of the future and what he could do."

Lauren was also dreaming of making more money. His job at Daniel Hays only paid about $50 a week, and another part-time job selling perfumes did not earn him much more. Ed Brandau stepped in to help. He called a friend named Abe Rivetz, who made ties in Boston, Massachusetts. Rivetz had often talked about expanding his business to New York. Brandau suggested that he hire Lauren to sell Rivetz ties in New York. Rivetz agreed, and Lauren joined the company in January of 1964.

LAUREN STANDS OUT

From the start, Lauren stood out at Abe Rivetz, but not always in a good way. The tie industry was extremely conservative. "Everything was done by the book," wrote Lauren biographer Jeffrey Trachtenberg. "There was a right way and a wrong way to show a tie, write an order, color a tie. This was a snobby little world and what it didn't understand, it ignored. Fashion meant tradition, consistency was a virtue. Change in this business was measured in eighths of an inch."

Rivetz's sales force was not very impressed with Lauren when he arrived at the company. First of all, he was 20 years younger than all the other salesmen and had much less experience in the industry than they did. Also, Lauren had come from the glove industry and knew nothing about how to make and sell ties. Then there was Lauren's wardrobe. Instead of conservative suits, Lauren wore shirts with wide collars and jackets that flared out from the body. It all seemed too flamboyant for the other salesmen. "I was a young hungry guy who lived in the city and said, 'Listen, this is what's happening,'" Lauren said. "The guys at Rivetz didn't understand it. It wasn't Boston."

Other people in the industry began to notice Lauren's unusual styles. On May 21, 1964, the menswear industry trade paper *Daily News Record* ran a full-page article about him. The article was titled "The Professional Touch" and described several of Lauren's distinctive clothes and included sketches of them. The other salesmen at Rivetz were stunned at the attention. They could not understand why anyone would care about what this upstart young salesman was wearing.

Abe Rivetz's son-in-law, Mel Creedman, was one of the people who never understood Lauren's style or attitude. "Ralph was different," Creedman said. "If everybody was clean shaven, Ralph wore a beard. When the industry was selling skinny ties, Ralph had to wear a wide one." Another salesman, Robert Stock, thought Lauren "looked like somebody from outer space."

Rivetz, on the other hand, liked Lauren and thought he was something special. He understood Lauren's desire to stand out from the crowd. Even though Rivetz was 40 years older than Lauren, he had the same imagination and attitude. "Abe understood me," Lauren once said. "He had that little extra, that hunger. We

ELEMENTS OF STYLE

The necktie industry was full of men wearing hats, old men, and it was a very dead industry. I came along, and I had a sports car and a tweed jacket..

--*Ralph Lauren in* Genuine Authentic *by Michael Gross*

were close." Rivetz even started going to the same tailor that Lauren used and wearing the same style of suits.

There was one thing Rivetz could not put up with, and that was Lauren's car. At the time, Lauren drove a sporty British car called a Morgan. The car was elegant, but it was so small, it did not have a trunk. That meant that when Lauren went on sales calls, he had to store all his sample ties in a tiny space behind the front seat, where they could easily be seen by anyone passing by. The situation really bothered Abe Rivetz, and he demanded that Lauren "get a salesman's car, a car with a trunk that locks." Lauren gave in and sold his car, replacing it with another sporty car—but one that did have a trunk.

LAUREN IN LOVE

The year 1964 was an important one for Ralph professionally. It was also an exciting time in his personal life. A few months before

The Influence of British Fashion

By 1964, fashion in Great Britain had changed tremendously from the conservative look of the 1950s. Young designers began opening small stores, or boutiques, in London's Knightsbridge, Kings Road, and Carnaby Street neighborhoods. Men and women who had once bought clothes at department stores or had their clothes made for them by tailors flocked to these new stores to try the latest styles. "Anything goes" became the motto for the 1960s, as new styles such as wide ties, brightly colored shirts and suits for men, and miniskirts, patterned tights, and hot pants for women, became popular.

People were also inspired by rock stars and movie stars, who often wore outlandish clothes that were quickly copied and distributed to the public. It did not take long before these new styles and ideas crossed the Atlantic and became popular in the United States as well.

After meeting at an eye doctor's office, Lauren and Ricky Low-Beer realized how much they had in common and fell in love. Following a brief courtship, the two were married in 1964.

joining the Abe Rivetz Company, Lauren had met a young receptionist in his eye doctor's office. The receptionist's name was Ricky Low-Beer. Ricky was six years younger than Lauren, and Lauren was struck by her tall, blonde beauty. Later, Lauren said he had fallen in love with Ricky at first sight. "She was very European," he said. "She was an only child and very sheltered. She was unlike any American girl I'd seen. She told me she liked me because I was dressed like one of her Viennese uncles, a wealthy man who has his suits made at the famous Viennese tailor Knize."

Ricky and Lauren had a lot in common. Like Lauren, Ricky's family was Jewish and had immigrated to the United States to escape hard times. They had left Austria to escape Adolf Hitler's persecution of the Jews. The family had lived in Shanghai, China, until 1942, when Japan declared war on China, and they fled to safety in the United States. Ricky was born in the United States in 1945.

Ricky and Lauren both loved to dance and often went to a club in the Gotham Hotel. The club was glamorous and featured "new" European music by groups like the Beatles. The couple also went out to dinner at Italian restaurants. Lauren discovered that, not only was Ricky fun to talk to and be with, she also believed in him and his dreams. After a short courtship, Lauren asked Ricky to marry him.

The couple married on December 20, 1964, at a catering hall in the Bronx. Lauren was twenty-five years old, and Ricky was nineteen. After a short honeymoon, the couple settled into a small one-bedroom apartment in a building just a few blocks from where Lauren's parents lived. Lauren's father painted the apartment, and the newlyweds decorated it with pictures they cut out of magazines and cheap furniture they bought at discount stores. After their honeymoon, Lauren went back to work at Rivetz. Things, however, were about to change at that company in a big way.

4

The Birth of Polo

When Lauren went back to work, he received some very bad news. Abe Rivetz, his boss and mentor, had died the day Lauren and his new wife returned home from their honeymoon. Without Rivetz to champion him, every day at Rivetz became a battle Lauren could not win.

A NEW BOSS

After Rivetz died, his son-in-law, Mel Creedman, took over the company. Creedman and Lauren had never gotten along, and their relationship did not improve after Creedman became his boss.

Fashion was changing, but Lauren seemed to be the only one at Rivetz to see the future. "It was a time in America to change," he said. "It was a time to break the rules." Lauren pestered Creedman relentlessly to allow him to design a line of ties. Finally, Creedman and his head salesman, Phineas Connell, let Lauren design prints and color combinations for a company that sold fabric to Rivetz. The results did not make anyone happy.

"We let him have his head, but he was premature, too far ahead, too wide, too wild," Connell said. "He was costing us money. It wasn't our trade. I had a terrible time with him."

Lauren was so sure that his ideas would be a success that he actually cried when Connell rejected one of his color combinations. Lauren saw that fashion was changing in Europe, and that people were getting their inspirations from the wild colors and patterns worn by rock stars, movie stars, and other celebrities. Lauren believed that the conservative look, then popular in America—narrow ties in dark colors and small, boring patterns—was a look that was dying out. People wanted something new, something different, and Lauren knew they would welcome a designer who created what they wanted.

Lauren was also afraid someone else would beat him to creating a new look. "I started to see that I had a lot of good ideas and they [the Rivetz salesmen] did not listen to me and six months later the ideas I had would pop up in someone else's line, so I said, 'Hey, I could have done it.'"

Lauren also tried to convince Mel Creedman that people would be willing to pay a higher price for his ties. Creedman found the idea ridiculous. He refused to believe that consumers would pay more for an "exclusive" look. Creedman did not doubt that Lauren had some good ideas, but he did not think these ideas would be relevant to the customers of the time. "Ralph wanted to do everything except what our customers wanted. The world is not ready for Ralph Lauren," Creedman said.

OPPORTUNITY KNOCKS

Lauren continued to work at Rivetz for another two years, though he later said that "it felt like more than that. I was very frustrated. I had to go." He knew, however, that he could never fulfill his dream

In the 1970s, celebrities like Alain Delon *(above)* helped inspire exciting trends in European menswear while American fashion remained muted and traditional. Lauren, who had tried to incorporate a more European look at Rivetz, left the company when they rejected his ideas.

while working there, so he began to look for another opportunity. The answer seemed obvious to Lauren and his wife, Ricky. Lauren should start his own business.

Starting a business required a lot of money, which Lauren did not have. He searched for someone to invest in him, or provide money for him to get started, but no one was interested. Lauren told everyone he knew that he was looking for investors. Finally, in 1967, Lauren's hard work paid off. Ned Brower, the owner of the Beau Brummel neckwear company, agreed to sell Lauren's ties.

Beau Brummel's ties were conservative and skinny, nothing like Lauren's wide, colorful designs, but Brower thought that was a good thing. "Ned was looking to give somebody a break, and that's what happened," said his widow, Shirley Brower. Lauren's ties would complement the Beau Brummel line, not compete with it. He offered Lauren his own division and told the younger man he had the freedom to do everything himself. "Ned let Ralph do it his own way, as far as creating was concerned," Shirley Brower explained. Lauren happily quit his job at Rivetz and went to work for himself.

Now that he had his own line, Lauren needed to name it. He talked with his friends, his brother Jerry, who also worked in the garment industry, and with Ned Brower. Lauren wanted a name that was both sporty and elegant. Finally, he settled on "Polo," naming his line after a sport that had been popular among royalty and the upper classes for many years. "I could not call it basketball or base-ball," Lauren later explained. Polo had "an international quality, a sense of Europe, a sense of elegance. It had an ambiance of style, so it was sports mixed with style and lifestyle." Lauren also liked that the name was short and easy to remember. "Glamorous, international, and playboyish," he said. "That's how the whole story started."

A ONE-MAN BUSINESS

Lauren's first office was a tiny back room in Beau Brummel's New York office in the Empire State Building. Lauren's office had no windows, and it was so small he had to keep all of his ties and samples in his desk.

Lauren did all the work for his new business. Despite the hard work, it was a dream come true. Lauren devoted himself to finding fabric in bright colors and unique patterns. He explored thrift shops, street vendors, and stores that sold fabric remnants. Lauren did not care if the material he found had been used to make couch upholstery or something other than clothes, as long as it had the right pattern and colors.

After Lauren designed the ties, he found a tailor named George Bruder to make them. Lauren's obsession with details sometimes frustrated Bruder, but he liked Lauren and had the patience to make his vision a reality. "I don't know how he got his ideas," Bruder later said of Lauren. "He was really different. If he saw your coat and liked it, he'd say, 'Let's make a tie out of it.'" At night, Lauren, his wife, and Ricky's mother would sit around the kitchen table, sewing Polo labels onto the ties.

The History of Ties

Men have worn cloth around their necks for thousands of years. The earliest evidence of men wearing ties came in 221 B.C., when the Chinese emperor Shih Huang Ti buried an army of terra-cotta statues in his tomb. Each of the life-sized soldiers was wearing a tie. Ties became popular in Europe after soldiers in Croatia wore scarves as part of their uniform. The French copied the style and called the neckwear a "cravat," which came from the word *Croat*. Over the years, cravats became narrower and straighter and became known as ties because the fabric was tied in a knot around the neck. By the 1950s, ties had become thinner and plainer, but a wider and more colorful style became popular in the 1960s and continues today.

Once Lauren had his samples, he had to go out and sell them. Most people agreed that Lauren was a very talented salesman. When Lauren was presenting ties, he picked each one up individually, rubbed the fabric, and talked about the ties as if they were the most beautiful and special creations on earth. Lauren biographer Jeffrey Trachtenberg wrote: "Ralph made his listeners see his ties the way he did, as more than ordinary pieces of cloth. . . . Years later, men who'd worked as salesmen their entire adult lives would marvel at Ralph's ability to romance a line. Ralph wanted others to share the image of the world as he saw it, and for those few minutes, when he talked, they did."

A SMALL START

Lauren's ties were expensive to make, but that did not bother him. At a time when most ties sold for $3 or $4, Lauren priced his ties at $7.50 to $15.00. Lauren also knew his best bet was to sell his ties in just a few high-end stores so they would be exclusive items. He did not want Polo ties to be something a shopper could find anywhere.

Slowly, Lauren found a few store owners who agreed to stock his ties. He was especially pleased when a store named Paul Stuart started selling his ties. Lauren bought many of his own clothes at Paul Stuart and knew that having his ties there would open the doors to other markets. Lauren also sold ties to another exclusive store, Meledandri. Although these sales were not big, they gave Lauren bragging rights and impressed other stores.

Lauren's strategy worked. Soon fashionable stores such as Louis of Boston and Eric Ross were stocking Lauren's ties. His ties were a big success among a select group of men who wanted to be at the forefront of the new fashion. Berny Schwartz, who stocked Lauren's ties in his Eric Ross menswear store in Beverly Hills, California, said, "Wearing a Ralph Lauren tie in those days was like belonging to a fraternity. No matter who you saw and where you saw them, you were identified as a fraternity brother. It could be on a plane, in an elevator, but when you saw someone wearing one of his ties, you smiled."

One of Lauren's early successes came when Neal Fox, a buyer for the upscale department store Neiman Marcus, visited New York and met with Lauren. He was so impressed he encouraged Lauren to send some of his samples to the main office in Dallas, Texas. Instead of mailing the samples, Lauren got on a plane and delivered them personally. He did so because "I knew the buyer wouldn't understand my ties unless I explained them in person." Lauren's unusual method paid off. He returned to New York with an amazing order from Neiman Marcus for one hundred dozen ties, his largest sale to date.

BREAKING INTO BLOOMINGDALE'S

Lauren's success with Neiman Marcus made him want an even bigger market. For years, he had dreamed of selling his ties to Bloomingdale's, the most famous and fashionable store in New York. He was unable, however, to break into the tight-knit world of Bloomingdale's sales force.

Lauren had a good friend named Joe Aezen, who was a salesman for another tie company called Rooster. Aezen was loud and wild, but store buyers really liked him. Aezen was never quiet about things he liked, and he really liked Lauren's designs. So whenever Aezen visited Bloomingdale's, he would bring samples of Lauren's ties. Jack Schultz, who was then one of Bloomingdale's buyers, recalled how persistent Aezen was about Lauren's ties. "Bloomingdale's probably wouldn't have recognized Ralph Lauren's talent without Joe Aezen's help."

Finally, Bloomingdale's decided to give Lauren a chance. Their offer, however, had two conditions Lauren could not agree to. Bloomingdale's wanted Lauren to make his tie a quarter of an inch narrower, and they wanted the ties to carry the Bloomingdale's name instead of the Polo name. Lauren said no.

Lauren's boss, Ned Brower, was angry with Lauren. He reminded Lauren that he was supposed to be making money for the company, and that he would never achieve that if he turned down such a major account. At the time, Lauren had only sold his ties to about two dozen stores. Still, Lauren held firm. His goal and his beliefs were more important to him than making a sale.

A GROWING REPUTATION

Despite the disappointing experience with Bloomingdale's, Lauren's reputation was growing in the industry. Along with selling his ties in exclusive, high-end stores, he also gave interviews to many different fashion journalists who were fascinated by this young man with bold new ideas.

Lauren received a lot of press from *Daily News Record*, a fashion news magazine. The paper's staff often took Lauren to lunch and included items about him and his ties in the magazine.

Lauren received even greater exposure when he made friends with Robert Green, the men's fashion editor at *Playboy* magazine. Green was an influential man who often appeared on popular television talk shows. Lauren heard that Green was happy to meet with new designers, so he called up the editor and asked to see him.

Green later recalled Lauren's phone call. "Ralph called me, and he was very young," he said. "He was this nervous little voice on the telephone, a voice so nervous that I became immediately sympathetic." Green agreed to stop by Lauren's office and look at his ties. He was stunned by what he saw. Green had seen wide ties by London designers before, but this was something different. "What Ralph had done was take fabrics not associated with neckwear design and make them into ties. Suddenly you were looking at extraordinary madders and paisleys, almost landscape designs. Well, I went berserk."

Green wanted to show Lauren's work to the world. He featured Lauren's ties in a *Playboy* feature on men's fashion. Lauren's ties appeared on the same pages as designs by noted fashion designers

When Bloomingdale's asked Lauren to alter his designs and sell his ties under the store's name, Lauren declined their offer. Shortly afterward, fashion critics began noticing his ties when shopping at other high-end stores.

such as Bill Blass and Pierre Cardin. The fashion world and the department stores took notice. Lauren's time was coming.

A DREAM COME TRUE

In the spring of 1968, Bloomingdale's approached Lauren once again about selling his ties in their stores. This time, it was not Gary Shafer in the Manhattan store who negotiated with Lauren. A buyer in a Bloomingdale's store in Fresh Meadows in the New York City borough of Queens wanted to carry Lauren's ties. Sales at the store exploded, and the Manhattan office took notice. Soon the Manhattan store began selling Lauren's ties, and this time they did not ask for any changes to the design or the name.

ELEMENTS OF STYLE

If you buy expensive products you don't want to see them all over the place. You want to know what you are getting is a rarity. I still believe that.

--Ralph Lauren in Genuine Authentic *by Michael Gross*

Lauren was thrilled to finally be in Bloomingdale's on his own terms. He was so proud that he set up the display himself. He personally put each tie into the display and showed the salesmen exactly how they should be knotted and laid out. He even stopped by during the week to straighten the cases.

Lauren's ties sold well. On Father's Day 1968, the Bloomingdale's store on Lexington Avenue in New York set up a special display of his ties. Lauren was so excited that he went to the store and polished the glass case himself. Frank Simon, the men's merchandising manager, was very pleased with the display. "Those ties were wide and controversial," he said, "and they looked wonderful to me because they represented a new direction. They were out of the mainstream, but the fabrics were of the finest material. Ralph insisted on quality. He also insisted on the prices, which I thought were too high. I was wrong."

Lauren had achieved his dream, but now he had an even bigger goal in mind. After just a year in business, he told the *Daily News Record*, "My long-range wish would be to design all kinds of men's wear, not just ties." Lauren believed that what he did for ties could also be done for shirts, pants, and sweaters. For Lauren, ties were only the beginning.

5

A Menswear Empire

y 1968, Lauren's ties were becoming hugely popular, and Lauren was ready to take the next step and design other items of clothing. He faced, however, several more hurdles on his road to success.

A NEW COMPANY

Although Lauren was pleased at his increasing success, his boss, Ned Brower, was not very impressed. Brower was losing patience with Lauren's refusal to sell his ties to stores he did not think were exclusive enough. After Lauren refused large orders from Wallach's, a chain of men's stores, and the department store chain Macy's, Brower began to wonder if Lauren had any business sense at all. Lauren, however, felt he had made the right decision. He firmly believed that if people could get a product in any store, that product would not be unique or valuable anymore. Brower was more concerned with money and profits. All he knew was that Lauren's ties were not making money and he would have much better profits if he sold the Polo line in a larger market. Lauren's friends felt that Brower just did not understand Lauren. Jack Schultz of Bloomingdale's said, "Brower didn't get what Lauren was proposing. Lauren was about style, not profit."

In 1968, Lauren received an interesting offer from a suit manufacturer named Norman Hilton. Hilton's suits were of a high quality, and Lauren had admired them for a long time. Hilton became interested in Lauren when he noticed that "people who were really hip began showing up with beautiful fat ties." Hilton was impressed when he met Lauren. "He was already a winner," he said of Lauren. "He was highly thought of by the best retailers in America."

Hilton was looking for someone to design ties and shirts to go with the Hilton line of suits. Like Lauren, Hilton believed in selling a total "look"—a line of fashions that could be worn together. Hilton asked Lauren if he would like to work for him. Just as he had done with Bloomingdale's first offer, Lauren said no. Lauren did not want to work for anyone else. He wanted his own company.

The two men parted on friendly terms. Hilton continued to be impressed by Lauren's sense of style. A few months later, the two men met again. This time, Hilton offered financial backing for Lauren to start his own company. Hilton lent the younger man $50,000. In exchange, Hilton would receive half ownership of Lauren's new business.

Before he could start his own business, Lauren had to settle his affairs with Ned Brower. Brower allowed Lauren to keep his Polo name and the trademark of a polo player on a horse. Brower also sold Lauren all the ties and fabrics Lauren had been using. The two men remained friends for years afterward. Lauren often sent Brower custom-made Polo items. After Brower died, Lauren sent his widow a letter that read: "Everything I am today, I can thank Ned Brower for."

Lauren purchased the Polo name and trademark—a polo player atop a horse—to use in his new company. This image is sewn onto every piece of Ralph Lauren clothing and has become iconic in the fashion industry.

On October 18, 1968, Polo Fashions was incorporated as a legal company in New York State. Even before that date, Lauren was visiting stores and taking orders. He wore the first Polo suits, which he had made for him by a tailor named Jimmy Palazzo. "The original samples were made to fit him," Palazzo said. "He wore the clothes to the stores so he could sell them. He got his initial orders because of that."

Just four days after Polo incorporated, Lauren made his debut as a suit designer at a fashion show at New York's prestigious Plaza Hotel. Lauren showed a suit with just one button on the jacket, wide lapels, pleated pants, and a big, fat tie. His formfitting, tailored suit looked very different from the baggy, oversized suits that were in fashion at the time. Lauren stood out. The show also put him in the company of some of the day's top designers, including Oleg Cassini, Bill Blass, and Pierre Cardin.

TECHNICAL TROUBLES

Lauren's suits looked great and got glowing reviews. There was just one problem. Lauren had no technical skills. Unlike most designers, Lauren had never learned how to sketch a design and transform that design into a pattern for a tailor to use to make the actual suit. At the same time, Lauren was obsessed with every detail and refused to make any compromises. He had many furious arguments with Michael Cifarelli, the tailor who was the head of Hilton's suit factory. Norman Hilton recalled one argument over the shoulders on a suit jacket. "Cifarelli took the jacket off the form, carefully. Then he began to jump up and down on it with his feet. . . . So you can see it was a little difficult."

The fighting continued until the first batch of suits was shipped to Bloomingdale's. The suits were a disaster. The pants were too long and did not fit right in the waist. The sleeves of the jackets were much too short. Bloomingdale's sent the entire shipment back. Hilton blamed Lauren for the problem, while Lauren blamed Hilton and his workers.

From Sketch to Clothing

Designing and producing an article of clothing involves several steps. First the designer usually sketches his or her idea on a piece of paper. The designer next takes a sample of material and drapes it over a dress form to see if it fits right. Next the designer or a pattern maker creates a pattern on paper that details exactly how long and wide the garment is, where the seams will be, and other details. A sample garment is made and tried on by a model to see how the garment looks on a real person. Once the designer is happy with his or her creation, it is sent to a factory to be made into clothes that will appear in stores a few months later.

INSPIRATIONS . . . AND PROBLEMS

Despite the problems, Hilton still had faith in Lauren. He knew that the designer just needed more experience. In the spring of 1969, Hilton asked Lauren to go to Italy on a buying trip. For Lauren, the trip was an eye-opener. He had never been to Europe and was astonished at the different fashions and merchandise available in Italy, then one of the most influential fashion centers in the world. Lauren shopped in the finest stores in Rome and studied the way people dressed.

Lauren did not stop studying fashion even when he was eating dinner. His traveling companion, Ed Brandau, recalled one memorable meal. "One evening we went out to eat at a chic underground restaurant," Brandau explained. "Ralph called the waiter over. The waiter didn't speak English, and Ralph didn't speak Italian. But Ralph made himself understood. What he wanted was the white laundry coat the man was wearing. And he finally got it."

Lauren bought the jacket right off the waiter's back. He admired the jacket's simple lines and loose fit, as well as its lack of padding and heavy seams. To him, the jacket looked like a favorite shirt, one a man wanted to wear again and again. The jacket would be Lauren's inspiration for his next line of suits.

When Lauren returned to New York, he immediately got to work on his new collection, which featured unconstructed jackets and suits modeled after the loose-fitting waiter's jacket he had bought in Italy. Lauren planned to sell his new suit at Bloomingdale's for the price of $125. That was a lot lower than the usual price of a Lauren suit, but it would appeal to young professionals who enjoyed shopping and wanted to look stylish.

Unfortunately, Lauren's line of unconstructed clothes was a huge flop. Men did not want a jacket that fit like a shirt. This time, Lauren did not have a sense of how people wanted to dress. The line sold so poorly that it quickly disappeared from the stores.

Around this time, Lauren met an Italian tailor named Leo Lozzi, who worked for a company called Lanham. Unlike Michael Cifarelli at Hilton, Lozzi instantly understood the type of look

Lauren wanted and how to create it. Lozzi said, "Ralph Lauren is a man who talks very little. He is not a clothing man, he's a man with a vision. You have to understand it. . . . I am not a genius but I understood Ralph right away. Ralph and I communicated without talking. . . . Ralph wanted a garment to look such a way . . . without explaining how, because he couldn't, but he made gestures with his hands . . . rounder, softer, a longer lapel, high pockets, shaped. . . . I understood what he wanted."

Lauren was thrilled to finally find a tailor who understood what he wanted. In the summer of 1970, he moved all his clothing production from Hilton's factory to Lanham's. Norman Hilton was furious, but Lauren refused to change his mind. As always, he wanted things done his way.

GOOD NEWS

In spite of his professional difficulties, Lauren experienced many joyous events during this time. On May 7, 1969, Lauren's wife gave birth to their first son, Andrew. Ricky Lauren had been pregnant when Lauren went on his trip to Italy, and he had been reluctant to leave her. The birth of their first child brought great happiness to both new parents.

In 1970, Lauren received major recognition from the fashion industry when he won the prestigious Coty Award for the best menswear designer. The Coty American Fashion Critics' Award had been created in 1943 by Eleanor Lambert, who worked for Coty Cosmetics and thought that sponsoring a fashion award would bring prestige and attention to the cosmetics company. The Coty Award soon became the Academy Award of the design world and was considered the highest honor a designer could achieve. Until 1969, awards were only given to the designers of women's fashions. This practice changed in the late 1960s as more designers began creating men's fashions. A prize for menswear design was added in 1969, and the first winner was Bill Blass.

Bill Blass *(above, with Lauren)* was already an established, celebrated designer in the 1970s when Lauren's ties started to gain attention. Blass was the first designer to receive the Coty Award for menswear.

Everyone was amazed when Lauren became only the second menswear designer to win the award when he was honored in 1970. He had only been in business for two years, and winning an award so early in his career was very unexpected. Joe Barrato, Polo's sales manager at the time, remembered the excitement. "When Eleanor [Lambert] called to tell us we'd won the Coty, we went crazy. It was like a dream. It was that exciting."

ANOTHER BATTLE WITH BLOOMINGDALE'S

Winning the Coty Award pushed Lauren into the ranks of America's top designers and earned him more respect among buyers and other industry representatives. It also helped him when he had to face down Bloomingdale's for the second time in his career.

Lauren wanted Bloomingdale's to open a Ralph Lauren shop within its store. The shop would be like a special boutique that carried all the different types of clothes Lauren was now making. At the time, this merchandising idea was unheard of. No designer had tried to sell all of his or her different lines in one place. Ties were sold in the tie department, and suits were sold in the suit department. Lauren had a different idea. He wanted to give his customers choices for every part of their wardrobes, from suits to wear to work to casual clothes to wear on weekends, and have all those items available in one place so shoppers could see how they all worked together. He was selling an image and a way of life, not just suits and ties.

Frank Simon at Bloomingdale's thought Lauren's idea was ridiculous. He thought that grouping all the Polo items together would hurt sales in other parts of the store. Lauren refused to give in. He told Simon that if Bloomingdale's did not build a shop for him, he would take his clothes and sell them somewhere else. "That's Ralph," Simon said. "He's a good, cool negotiator, and he's consistent." Simon gave in.

The Ralph Lauren Polo Shop opened on Bloomingdale's main floor in the fall of 1971. It was the first time Bloomingdale's

---

ELEMENTS OF STYLE

There is a foundation of taste that has flair. What I do is feel things. I like classics. . . . I saw the world as a much bigger world, not a narrow regimented world. I did what I felt was exciting for the time. And I felt change was needed. I dressed nothing like the people who influenced me. . . . They influenced me but I didn't look like them. That was the difference.

—*Ralph Lauren in* Ralph Lauren: The Man Behind the Mystique
by Jeffrey A. Trachtenberg

men's department had given a designer his own space. Frank Simon still was not sure this was a good idea. "We don't really believe in 'designer clothing,'" he said in a *New York Times* article soon after the boutique opened. In the same article, Lauren countered, "I don't believe in it myself. I make clothes I like to wear."

What Lauren wanted was what his customers wanted. The Ralph Lauren Polo Shop was a huge success. Grouping his designs together increased sales of all the items. Once again, Lauren was right.

FAMILY MAN

In 1971, Lauren became a father for the second time with the birth of his son, David. Although he was a driven businessman, Lauren was also devoted to his family. He and Ricky spent as much time with their sons as possible. The couple attended parties, but the social scene was not really the center of their lives. "I want to be a star," Lauren told *Gentlemen's Quarterly*. "I don't want to go to a party and have to promote myself. I want to be recognized. But I want to be myself, too. You must try not to lose yourself."

Instead of going to parties, the Laurens took part in family activities. The whole family enjoyed sports and often took vacations together at the beach in the Hamptons on Long Island, New York. As his sons got older, Lauren also educated them about business. He treated his sons as intelligent young men who had valuable opinions. His son Andrew later told an interviewer, "My father always played the role of regular father . . . he was always there for dinner so we shared a lot of our youth with him. . . . My memory of my dad is not of a guy who was famous but the person whom I wrestled with and ran around with when I was a kid."

Lauren's other son, David, also spoke highly of his father. "Dad very rarely talked about business problems but he educated us from when we were little about everything he was doing. . . . We had very serious debates." Andrew and David were encouraged to ask questions and debate serious issues with their parents. Lauren wanted his sons to have the same sense of confidence and independence that he did.

6

Designing for Women

By 1972, Ralph Lauren was a big success in the world of men's fashion. Polo was doing almost $4 million a year in sales, and its profits at the end of 1971 were about $300,000. As always, however, Lauren had his eyes on a bigger prize. Lauren's new goal was to design clothes for women.

PLEASING RICKY

Lauren first became interested in designing for women because of his wife, Ricky. Ricky was petite and slim, and she often complained that she could not find clothes she liked when she went shopping. Lauren was sure that her frustration was shared by many other women. He decided to design clothes that fashionable women would want to wear.

Lauren had never designed anything for women, but he followed the same rules he used when designing for men. He was sure women wanted classic clothes made of high-quality materials that looked good and felt comfortable. Lauren loved the way Ricky looked when she wore Lauren's own shirts around the house or on vacation. So he modeled his first women's shirts after the design he had been using for men.

Lauren designed a shirt that was cut like a man's shirt and had a white collar and white cuffs, just like men wore. Lauren used only the finest cotton, linen, and silk fabrics, and he made the shirts in bright colors, solid patterns, and stripes.

The shirts had one more detail that became very important. Lauren added his polo-player logo on the cuff of the shirt, along with a label that read "Polo by Ralph Lauren." The logo was placed on the cuff instead of on the shirt front to distinguish the line from other brands on the market, which placed their logos on the front of the garment.

Lauren added his name to the clothes because he saw that designers were gaining value. "I added Ralph Lauren, because at that point Pierre Cardin was coming into the fold, and Bill Blass," he explained. "And there was a menswear image starting, people were aware of me, and I wasn't known in the women's business, so I put Ralph Lauren on the label with Polo." It was a smart move that made Lauren's shirts seem even more exclusive. The price was exclusive, too. Lauren's shirts cost about $24 apiece, much more than the average woman's shirt of that time.

BAD NEWS AND GOOD NEWS

Lauren got into the women's wear field at the right time, when American designers were becoming more famous. Up until then, upper-class women had mostly worn clothes designed by Europeans in the fashion capitals of Paris, Rome, and London. In the

Lauren ventured into women's fashion at a time when an increasing number of women were entering the workforce. Looking for professional, stylish clothing, many of these new workers turned to Lauren's masculine blouses and suits.

early 1970s, however, American designers were making a name for themselves, and American women were eager to buy products designed specifically for them.

Lauren did face some challenges in his new line, however. Although there had been many men designing clothes for women, all of these designers had started in the women's wear market. Lauren was the first designer who tried to move from designing menswear to designing for women, and many people felt that he was doomed. These critics did not believe that American women would want to buy clothes that had been designed by a menswear designer. Polo salesman Ken Giordano explained, "You might say there was a lot of skepticism, because until then designers had first established themselves in the women's business and then moved into men's wear. We were doing the opposite. And there were a lot of things we didn't know."

A bigger problem was the way Lauren's new shirts fit. Most designers hired women called "fit models" to wear their samples to make sure they would fit the average woman. Lauren did not follow this tradition. Instead, he used his good friend and Polo's marketing director, Buffy Birrittella, as a model for his clothes. Birrittella was built the same way as Lauren's wife, Ricky—small and very thin. While the skinny, tight-fitting shirts looked great on Birrittella and Ricky, they did not fit the average American woman. Lauren knew his shirts would not fit most women, but he did not care. Polo salesman Ken Giordano said, "Ralph really only cared about one thing. He wanted to dress Ricky. As long as the clothes fit her, he was satisfied."

Kelli Questrom, who worked for Lauren and often wore her husband's shirts and recut his pants to fit her, explained:

> Ralph always envisioned certain kinds of bodies, certain kinds of personalities, as his perfect client, his perfect customer. He would say to me, "I dream of dressing Audrey Hepburn [a movie actress and style icon famous for her slim, boyish figure]. But

my client is never Audrey Hepburn, it's Irma." He was trying to make clothes for a streamlined body. He liked thin women. . . . So he'd pick a rail like me to see how the clothes would look on the customer he envisioned. But those customers seldom bought his clothes.

Bloomingdale's and other stores that carried Lauren's first line of women's shirts were initially concerned that their customers would hate them because of the poor fit. The stores were wrong. Fashionable women were so eager to wear the new Lauren line that they simply bought a larger size when their regular size did not fit them. Joe Barrato said, "They had to buy at least one size larger than normal. It wasn't good for them psychologically, but they wanted the shirts." Bloomingdale's flagship store in New York sold out of the shirts as soon as they went on sale. Once again, Lauren understood what women wanted and how to create it.

NEW LINES

Once Lauren succeeded with blouses, he moved on to other items of women's clothing. In May 1972, Lauren showed a women's collection that included a tweed suit with slim sleeves and a tapered waist and a gray suit with a high waist and cuffed pants, along with blazers, shirts, and pleated pants. The look was very tailored and professional. Once again, Lauren had his finger on

---

ELEMENTS OF STYLE

I didn't know anything about the women's business. I just went and had the clothes made in a men's factory. I said, "I want this suit made for my wife; scale it down." I shortened the jackets, made them slim, with skinny arms. They fit some women and others couldn't get into them.

—*Ralph Lauren in* Genuine Authentic *by Michael Gross*

The success of Lauren's women's wear line was a major financial boost to the company, allowing him to hire more staff to help develop his ideas and designs. Here he looks over fall ads with his staff.

the pulse of society. At the time, women were beginning to enter the workforce in large numbers, and they wanted to be taken seriously. One way to do that was to dress like a professional man, and Lauren's fashions allowed them to do just that. Lauren's designs also gave young women a way to rebel against traditional feminine styles in a sophisticated way. Lauren biographer Marvin Traub stated that, at the time, a woman wearing a man-tailored suit was an "acceptable way to express a sophisticated brand of nonconformism." Lauren offered women in the business world a way to look professional and stylish.

NEW INNOVATIONS

In 1972, Lauren also introduced two more new lines. The first, Chaps, featured moderately priced men's pants. It was common in the fashion industry for companies to create low-priced copies of popular styles. These copies were called knockoffs. The success of Polo knockoffs was no surprise to Lauren, but it annoyed him anyway. The knockoffs annoyed Bloomingdale's, too, because they took away from the store's Polo sales.

To compete with the cheap knockoffs, Lauren created Chaps. Lauren named the line after the leather pants worn by American cowboys, going back to the love of cowboy movies he had as a child. Chaps menswear was sold at Bloomingdale's and other major department stores and provided a lower-priced alternative to Lauren's classic but expensive Polo line. However, Lauren's first love would always be Polo. His biographer, Jeffrey

Women in the Workforce

Women had always worked, but for most of U.S. history they did not have high-ranking, decision-making positions. In the early 1970s, most working women held low-level jobs, and very few were managers or executives. There was discrimination against women because many people felt a woman's place was in the home. There was also a misleading belief that once women got married and had children, they would quit their jobs to raise families, which made many companies reluctant to hire women. The 1970s, however, brought a wave of feminism that opened the doors to different opportunities for women. Women slowly began to be hired for managerial positions and face a long, hard road of proving to their bosses and coworkers that they were just as serious about and capable of doing their jobs as men. For many women entering the business world, it was vital to be seen as equal to men. This led to the popularity of men-tailored clothes, such as suits, for working women all over America.

Dismissive of unimaginative clothes made from shoddy materials, Lauren only uses high-quality fabrics for his products. His collared knit shirts became so popular that the style is now known as polo shirts.

Trachtenberg, wrote that "Ralph Lauren created Chaps because it made business sense. He would market Chaps because that was what the stores wanted. But . . . Polo would always be first in his heart."

In the same year that Lauren introduced Chaps, he also introduced his signature Polo knit shirt. There were many other knit shirts on the market at the time, but they were made of lower-quality materials such as polyester or polyester-cotton blends. Lauren would have none of that. His shirts were made of 100 percent cotton that felt soft to the touch. Also, Lauren expanded the basic colors that were on the market. His shirts came in thirty bold colors. The Polo shirt became an instant classic and one of Lauren's best-selling lines. Today, that style of knit shirt is called a polo shirt.

STORM CLOUDS

The early 1970s were a time of huge growth for Lauren and Polo. Unfortunately, Polo was still a small company with a limited staff, overseen by Ralph Lauren himself. Although it sounds like good fortune for a small company to have big sales, meeting the huge demand while still delivering quality goods can be an impossible challenge. By the end of 1972, storm clouds were gathering on Lauren's horizon—dark clouds that could destroy everything he had worked so hard to achieve.

7

Financial Difficulties

As Polo grew rapidly in the early 1970s, Ralph Lauren seemed to be on top of the world. The quick growth, however, added to the problems that had been around since the beginning of the company and were about to combine into a disaster.

TIGHT SCHEDULES

Lauren had always had problems with manufacturing and shipping goods on time. In the early days, his inexperience with creating patterns and sample garments had led to entire shipments being rejected by stores because they arrived too late. No store wanted to sell winter coats in the middle of summer, or summer clothes in the dead of winter. Lauren's demand that every item be perfect did not help either. Michael Bernstein, who was hired as Polo's treasurer in

1971, remembered a time when Lauren went to his shirt factory and stopped production just to make the collar of the shirt a little bit longer. Another company officer, Ivan Benjamin, complained, "We could sell anything we wanted. But we couldn't get it made, or we couldn't get it made on time. . . . If your shipping window is January 25 to March 25 complete, and if you are still shipping goods the first of May, some guys refuse to accept it."

Matters only got worse when Lauren started making clothes for women. While menswear has two seasons, spring and fall, women's wear has four. Lauren had to come up with brand-new designs and produce clothes for spring, summer, fall, and holiday resort wear in winter. Creating every collection meant coming up with new designs, new fabrics, new styles, and new colors, not to mention the time it took to create patterns and send them to a factory to be produced. Lauren hired more staff to handle all the details, which increased his costs of doing business.

CASH FLOW

Lauren was also having trouble with cash flow. In any business, it is important that enough cash come in through sales to cover the costs of doing business. This was not happening at Polo. Lauren faced huge expenses to buy the material and other goods to make his products, pay his staff, pay rent and other costs for his offices and factories, and many other expenses. To cover expenses, Lauren, like many other businessmen, borrowed money. However, borrowing money meant repaying it on time or facing huge interest payments, which added more debt to the business. Most companies keep records to predict and track their cash flow, but Polo had no systems in place to manage those details. No one really knew how much money was coming in and how much was going out.

Polo should have been able to cover its expenses with the money it made from selling clothes. However, the company's cash flow model was not working. The stores that sold Lauren's clothes were supposed to pay him based on sales, but Lauren did not

Like his menswear, Lauren's women's wear featured classic, elegant styles with a touch of whimsy, like this plaid evening gown and cashmere coat. His high standards and expensive materials delayed production and caused money problems.

receive that money until months after he had borrowed money to make and ship the clothes to the stores. Some of the smaller stores had their own financial problems and did not pay him at all. And if delivery problems caused merchandise to arrive at a store too late to be sold that season, the store would reject the shipment, which meant more lost sales.

HELP FROM A FRIEND

For years, Lauren had been proud of the fact that he ran the business basically by himself. "I handled everything in the beginning," he said. But after a while, "I couldn't do all of it. I needed more sophistication to grow. I needed somebody there with me, working. . . . Things change and you have to grow." Lauren knew that he did not have the skills or the time to manage such a rapidly growing company. It was time to bring in a money man.

Lauren hired an old friend named Michael Bernstein to be the treasurer of Polo. "What I did was bring in a financial guy to run the part of the business that I didn't know how to do. I brought him in; nobody asked me to. I was willing to give him a piece of my business. I felt I needed him, and I did," Lauren explained.

Michael Bernstein had grown up in the same Bronx neighborhood as Lauren, and they had played basketball together when they were teenagers. Bernstein had graduated from City College and worked as an accountant. In February 1968, Bernstein was

---

ELEMENTS OF STYLE

I just grew too fast and was doing too many things at once and my cash flow was tight, and it was bad planning, bad organization, and there was a period when a recession hit. My business was great in stores but financially, it was tight.

—*Ralph Lauren in* Genuine Authentic *by Michael Gross*

made a partner at the accounting company, Max Rothenberg & Company. Bernstein specialized in working for businesses in the garment industry. Lauren had hired Max Rothenberg & Company to audit, or check, his financial affairs in 1970 and was so pleased with their work that he asked Bernstein to join Polo as its treasurer and chief financial officer when he needed help. Bernstein joined Polo in July of 1971. He realized almost immediately that he had walked into a lion's den.

A DOWNWARD SPIRAL

Bernstein had barely walked in the door for his first day on the job when he got a phone call from the First National Bank of Boston. This bank served as Polo's factor. A factor is a bank or other

Factors Versus Loans

Factors are different than loans. A loan is money that is given to a company. The company has to repay the loan over a certain period of time and usually pays interest, or extra money, for the privilege of borrowing the money in the first place. Factoring is a financial transaction where a business sells its accounts receivables to a third party called a factor. The company sells its invoices to the factor at a discount in exchange for immediate money with which to finance the business. For example, a company might have $100,000 in receivables, which it sells to a factor for $90,000. The factor will be repaid the $100,000 over time, eventually making a $10,000 profit. Factoring differs from a loan in that the company is not borrowing money but is selling a financial asset. In addition, while a loan involves only two parties—the company and the lender—factoring involves three parties—the company, the lender, and the businesses that owe the company money for goods or services.

financial organization that provides money to a business in order to finance production. The idea is that the factor's payment will allow a company to increase its inventory, and that inventory will eventually be sold to repay the loans. Unfortunately for Polo, and for Bernstein, the company owed the bank $300,000. That was more than Polo had earned the previous year and obviously more than they could repay.

The First National Bank was also concerned about Polo's returns. If a store returns clothes to the manufacturer, those clothes are not sold and they do not earn any money to repay the loan. The manufacturer then issues a chargeback, or credit, to the store for the unsold goods. Returns are a fact of life in any business, but Polo's chargebacks were much higher than they should have been. Bernstein later estimated that 13 percent of all Polo's shipped merchandise was returned, compared to an industry average of 3 to 6 percent. Between January and June 1971, Lauren racked up $100,000 in chargebacks. First National asked Bernstein to set up a meeting to discuss the problems immediately.

Bernstein's first day did not get any better. "There was no money for payroll that week," he realized. "No money in the bank. Can't pay bills. The bookkeeper is holding a substantial amount of checks. The business is out of control."

Bernstein did his best to manage the mess. He asked the company's officers to provide financial projections and keep strict records of all financial transactions. He also tried to crack down on uncontrolled spending. However, Lauren's staff, many of whom had been with him for years and were fiercely loyal to their boss, resented taking orders from a newcomer. Bernstein realized that he was not going to be able to save the company. "I tried to bring a toughness and a financial discipline that nobody wanted to adhere to," he complained.

Michael Gross, who wrote a biography of Lauren and has written extensively about the fashion industry, described the biggest problem. "By insisting on manufacturing women's shirts that didn't fit and were returned (as they were, in large numbers, by stores that didn't have a fashion victim clientele like Bloomingdale's), Polo was digging itself into a hole so deep, it would never climb out."

Bernstein and Lauren solved the immediate problem by getting a loan from another bank, Bankers Trust. However, Polo was still on shaky financial ground. Things only got worse when the company failed to pay federal withholding taxes for its employees on time and had to pay huge fines to the government as punishment.

Despite all the problems, Lauren was eager to buy out his business partner, Norman Hilton. After negotiating, Lauren agreed to pay Hilton $633,000 over several years, with $150,000 payable right away. Lauren was now the sole owner of the company, but he had to take out another loan to pay Hilton the money he owed him. Hilton really did not want to sell his share of Polo, and he felt Lauren was being greedy. "I like Ralph," he later told an interviewer. "He's got tremendous charm and all those things. But one of his major characteristics is greed. He's one of the greediest [men] you'll ever meet in your life." Hilton did concede that Lauren was a man of his word, however. "He was an absolute gentleman. I never thought I'd ever get the rest of the money, but I got every cent of it."

As Lauren's financial reputation got worse, so did his problems. Banks refused to lend him any more money. At the same time, contractors demanded cash payments for goods and services, asking for money the company did not have. Although Lauren's fashions were still getting great reviews from industry professionals, sales at both Polo and Chaps were down. By early 1973, Polo Fashions was on the verge of bankruptcy.

MAGUIRE SAVES THE DAY

It was clear Polo needed help, and Michael Bernstein found some. In January 1973, Bernstein found a new factor for the business. A company called John P. Maguire, Inc., came to the rescue. Maguire was a company that specialized in factoring. It bought out the debt Polo owed to Bankers Trust and took over as Lauren's lender. The new funding allowed Lauren's suppliers to continue selling material to him so Polo could keep running.

Dave Goldberg, the Maguire executive assigned to manage Lauren's account, immediately realized that the problems at Polo were bigger than anyone suspected. When Goldberg looked at the company's records, he realized that even though Polo had a substantial net worth, the company was out of cash. "It was a company out of control," he said. Even worse, since Lauren continued to sell clothes to accounts that could not pay him, much of the money the stores owed him was uncollectible. Still, Goldberg knew that Lauren had many things going for him. People in the industry supported him, and his products were in high demand. Goldberg was especially pleased that Bloomingdale's, Polo's biggest customer, wanted Lauren to stay in business. "Bloomingdale's made it clear they were going to stand behind him. Bloomingdale's support was important, because it showed us that somebody in fashion cared about him," Goldberg said.

Goldberg realized that Lauren had no idea how bad things were. After he went over the company's books, he drew up a new financial statement and showed it to Lauren. Lauren was shocked to realize that even though his company had increased its sales, it had no cash and was in debt for more than half a million dollars. "I remember the look on his face," Goldberg recalled. "I told him how close he was to losing everything—including his personal assets. It was like telling him he had cancer. He went pale. He was like a deer in the headlights."

Lauren also felt betrayed by Michael Bernstein. He felt that Bernstein had lied to him and had mismanaged the company by not letting Lauren know how much trouble they were in. He also did not like the fact that Bernstein seemed so surprised when Lauren confronted him about the company's problems. "You're running the business," Lauren complained. "I don't understand why you don't know. You're in charge of the finances. You're involved with the whole thing. I can't believe that you don't know, that it is a shock."

Lauren fired Bernstein on the spot. "He was in charge," Lauren said. "He had the financial role and I trusted him. . . . He was over his head and he didn't tell me." As far as Lauren was concerned, it was ridiculous for him to pay Bernstein to be the company's chief financial officer when Bernstein did not know if the company was losing money.

Bernstein was shocked by Lauren's actions and felt betrayed. He believed the company's problems were Lauren's fault, not his, but Lauren refused to argue with him. "I don't know what was in his mind," Bernstein later said. "'You're fired' was all he said." Bernstein was replaced with Lauren's brother Lenny.

A DIFFICULT PLAN

Fortunately for Lauren, Goldberg had some definite ideas on how to save the company. He drew up a list of five demands that Lauren would have to follow if Maguire was to remain as the company's factor. First, Lauren had to turn over his personal savings of about $100,000 to Maguire as a guarantee. The cash in that account would belong to Maguire and could not be taken by any other creditors. Lauren also had to renegotiate his debt and restructure his buyout payments to Norman Hilton. He had to ask for prepayments, or money up front, from his biggest accounts, including Bloomingdale's. Finally, Lauren had to license Chaps and the women's wear divisions to other companies. That meant Lauren would allow other companies to manufacture and market products with his name on them, in exchange for a fee.

Lauren was reluctant to follow all of Goldberg's demands, especially licensing his name. He was so worried, however, that he knew he had to agree, no matter how difficult it was. He realized that he was close to losing his company and his personal fortune. "That was the moment," he recalled. "It wasn't bankruptcy, but it was scary. I had to reorganize the company. I was living in the middle of a panic and I was in pain. But somehow I felt I wasn't going out of business and that it was going to be all right."

After receiving awards for his menswear, Lauren completed a difficult year on a high note when he won the 1973 Coty Award for women's wear, his first of many. *Above,* Lauren poses with Ricky and his award from the Council of Fashion Designers of America.

A NEW BEGINNING

In October 1973, Lauren signed a 10-year agreement with the Kreisler Group to license his women's wear business to them. Polo would receive $250,000 as a licensing fee, plus 5 to 7 percent of sales. Lauren would still design the clothes, but the Kreisler Group would purchase the materials, manufacture the clothes, and ship them to the accounts. This action helped Polo in two ways. It relieved the financial pressure of producing the women's wear line, and it injected much-needed cash into the company. Lauren also licensed the Chaps line in a similar agreement.

The changes Dave Goldberg had demanded paid off. Polo kept more accurate financial records and managed to pay its creditors on time even as business continued to expand. Operations were streamlined, and the licensing agreements created a reliable source of income. Goldberg was pleased with Polo's progress. Unfortunately, his bosses at John P. Maguire, Inc., disagreed. Polo was growing bigger, and Maguire knew that it would require a big increase in support to finance the company's expansion. Maguire did not want to extend itself to a company that it felt still had problems. In 1973, Maguire sent word to Lauren that its financial backing would end in 60 days. Luckily, Polo was able to find another factor very quickly when the United Virginia Factoring Company took over the account.

For Polo, the dark days were over. "By making our payments when we promised, we started to build credibility," said company officer Harvey Hellman. By March 1974, Polo was once again showing a profit.

That year brought more good things to Lauren. He won his third Coty Award, this time for designing clothes for women, not for menswear. Best of all, in May he became a father again, this time to a daughter named Dylan. It seemed that Lauren's future looked bright and he would soon be moving on to even bigger and better achievements.

8

The Sweet Smell
of Success

R alph Lauren ventured into many new areas in the next few years. From movie costumes to perfume, home furnishings to Ralph Lauren stores, the Ralph Lauren brand would be everywhere, influencing even more people around the world.

LAUREN GOES TO THE MOVIES

Lauren had always loved movies. As a child and teen, he had gone to the movies almost every Saturday and fantasized about becoming a cowboy. His love of movies continued as an adult. So he was really excited when a new opportunity came his way in 1973. Lauren was asked to manufacture some of the men's clothes for a new movie based on F. Scott Fitzgerald's classic novel, *The Great Gatsby*. The novel and movie were set on Long Island's exclusive North

Shore during the 1920s and featured the love lives and betrayals of wealthy characters.

Lauren loved the idea of combining movies with the elegant fashions of the 1920s, and he set to work creating concepts and designs to show to the film's costume designer, Theoni V. Aldredge. Aldredge chose the fabrics and designs she wanted based on the movie's story, and Lauren made the clothing to her specifications. Lauren was so pleased by Aldredge's ideas that he used some of the costume ideas when he created his next season of clothes. The movie's main character, Jay Gatsby, was someone Lauren admired because he was "a self-made man, and he was all about looking glamorous and wealthy and mysterious," according to Lauren, who must have seen a lot of similarities between Gatsby and himself.

Lauren was so thrilled by this assignment that he talked about it to the media. Fashion writers loved the story and gave Lauren a lot of publicity. Soon everyone had the impression that Lauren had designed the costumes for *The Great Gatsby*. This claim made Theoni V. Aldredge, the actual designer, very angry. Aldredge did not want anyone else to get credit for the job she was doing, and she pointed out that Lauren was simply manufacturing the clothes. "Manufacturers want to be involved for publicity, and we get the clothes for nothing," Aldredge explained. "I wouldn't have minded if Ralph Lauren said he manufactured some clothes. I minded that he said he designed the men's clothing. He thought he should have won an Academy Award for loaning me a dozen shirts!"

Aldredge was so angry she called Paramount Pictures, the studio that was making the film, and demanded that they take Lauren's men's wardrobe credit off the movie if he did not stop taking credit for something he had not done. Paramount refused, and Aldredge let the matter go . . . for a while. Aldredge, however, got a lot of satisfaction when she won an Academy Award for her costume design, nabbing the movie's only Oscar. When Aldredge went onstage to accept her award, she thanked many people involved in the movie, but never mentioned Ralph Lauren's name. Still, the experience was a good one for Lauren and his company. One of his executives explained that "*Gatsby* was a great moment for Lauren because it gave him the kind of recognition outside the industry that he had been seeking."

In 1977, Lauren worked on another movie. This time, he manufactured the costumes for Woody Allen's classic film *Annie Hall*. The film was based on a doomed romance between two New Yorkers, played by Allen and Diane Keaton. The movie became a classic not only because of its funny story line but also because of Keaton's costumes. Her character spent most of the movie wearing men's clothes, such as oversized shirts, vests,

Actress Diane Keaton wore Lauren's designs in the iconic New York movie *Annie Hall*. Her oversized, menswear-inspired clothing included one of his signature ties and became a major influence in women's fashion at the time.

and ties. Lauren provided the clothes to the movie's costumer. Keaton's look became an instant hit, and women everywhere copied the menswear look, giving Lauren another boost of publicity and sales.

LAUREN ENTERS THE FRAGRANCE BUSINESS

For many years, Lauren had been approached by different companies to put his name on fragrances. Fragrances created by fashion designers had a long and honorable tradition dating back to the iconic Coco Chanel in the 1920s. A good fragrance can make its wearer feel attractive and confident, just like a stylish outfit of clothing does. In addition, fragrances can be very profitable and sell well for many years. So it is no surprise that several companies wanted Ralph Lauren to create a fragrance for them.

Lauren, as usual, wanted to do things his way. His biggest concern was that his fragrance would be just one of many if he worked with a company that made many other fragrances. "I didn't want to be with a stable of people," Lauren said. "I wanted to build as the basis of the company, the way Estee Lauder was built as the basis of that company. I didn't want to be one of many but the only one. So I waited."

Finally, in 1976, Lauren got the deal he wanted. He signed with Warner Communications to sell and market two fragrances. Warner was involved in many different businesses, including music and publishing, and Lauren felt he could stand out by creating something new for Warner. Lauren also got along well with the Warner executives, especially David Horowitz, the company's executive vice president. Horowitz understood what Lauren wanted and how the deal could benefit him. "Ralph knew that there were only so many people who could afford to buy his clothing," Horowitz said. "Fragrances open a much wider world because they're low-cost items. Everybody could afford to own a piece of Ralph Lauren, to share in the aura."

Lauren agreed to create two fragrances for Warner. One, named Polo, would be for men, and the other, called Lauren, would be for women. According to the deal between the two companies, Warner owned the rights to the names and would handle all of the manufacturing details. Lauren would be responsible for approving the fragrances and designing the bottles they came in. In exchange, he would receive a 5 percent royalty, or a percentage of the profits, on every bottle sold.

AN ELEGANT BOTTLE

Just as he did designing clothes, Lauren took great care in designing the bottles that would hold his fragrances. Polo, the

Coco Chanel and Chanel No. 5

Gabrielle Chanel was born in France in 1883. Her childhood was filled with poverty and neglect. After her mother died, her father placed her in a Catholic orphanage, where the nuns taught her to sew. As a young adult, she sang in nightclubs and became known by the nickname Coco. Chanel set up her first shop selling hats in Paris in 1910. She also made her own clothes and began selling them after people asked her where she got her distinctive styles.

By 1922, Chanel's business was thriving. That year, she launched her first perfume, Chanel No. 5. Chanel said that perfume "is the unseen, unforgettable, ultimate accessory of fashion . . . that heralds your arrival and prolongs your departure." Chanel continued to design clothes that were both fashionable and comfortable. She created such iconic fashions as the Chanel suit, which featured a collarless jacket and a fitted skirt, and the "little black dress." Chanel died in Paris in 1971, but the company she started remains one of the most famous and popular design firms in the fashion world.

men's fragrance, was sold in a bottle shaped like an old-fashioned drinking flask. For the women's fragrance, Lauren got inspiration from his collection of Victorian inkwells. Lauren thought the inkwells were very romantic looking, so the Lauren fragrance was packaged in bottles shaped like old-fashioned inkwells. To tie the image of the two fragrances together, the Polo and Lauren bottles were all capped with a large gold top shaped like a doorknob. Of course, both bottles featured the company's distinctive polo player logo.

Although Lauren took great care in creating his designs, he soon ran into problems when it came to manufacturing and selling them. The first problem came in designing the inkwell-inspired bottle for Lauren. Most fragrance containers at the time had rounded edges because liquid flows more easily into rounded corners in a mold than it does into sharp corners. No American company could make the bottles the way Lauren wanted them to look, so Warner finally found a glass factory in Spain that could do the job. Making the bottles overseas meant the product cost more to produce and raised the price, but Lauren did not care. As always, he wanted a certain look, and he knew that people would be willing to pay extra for his idea.

Once the fragrances went on sale in March 1978, another, more dangerous, problem soon arose. Bottles began to explode in the department stores. Executives quickly figured out why. The perfume manufacturer had stored the fragrances outside in the cold, and when the sealed bottles were placed under the hot spotlights of a store display, the fragrance expanded and blew the tops off the bottles. The problem was easily fixed. Another problem occurred when the red color on the outside of the bottles started to peel off, but the factory was able to solve that problem quickly as well.

Despite the glitches, Lauren's perfumes sold extremely well. By 1987, nine years after their launch, Ralph Lauren fragrances were earning more than $6 million a year.

A critical element of Lauren's success lies in his instinct for predicting upcoming trends. From wide ties to cowboy chic, his designs have defined the looks of men and women for several decades.

NEW THEMES

Lauren was expanding more than just his business empire as the 1970s neared an end. He was also experimenting with new styles.

His 1978 fall women's wear collection featured Western-themed clothes. Although he had included some Western looks in his collections before, this time he emphasized the look. The models at his showcase that year wore suede-fringed leather jackets, puffy prairie skirts, satin cowboy blouses, jeans, and leather belts with silver cowboy buckles.

Fashion critics loved the new look. "Lots of New Collections, But Lauren Steals the Show," announced the *New York Times* in its review of the fall fashion show. *Women's Wear Daily*, a leading fashion magazine, ran an article headlined "Lauren: American Fantasies for Fall." In the article, a buyer for Bloomingdale's called the collection "a wonderful amalgam of all-American looks."

Stores all over the country were influenced by Lauren's collection. Jeffrey Trachtenberg explained, "Women were tired of the baggy, loose-fitting clothes most designers were then making here and in Europe. The customers also were wary of the big shoulder pads that were being shown as alternatives. Suddenly, American customers and retailers had something new to sell and hype."

Lauren continued to promote the Western look in later collections. After a vacation trip to New Mexico with his wife and children, he introduced his Santa Fe collection in 1982. This collection included items such as colorful prairie skirts, chamois skirts, turquoise jewelry, and wool sweaters inspired by Navajo Indian designs. The Santa Fe collection was hugely popular and was copied by many other designers.

ELEMENTS OF STYLE

America was my inspiration. Activities of life, not the activities of fashion. I was making that life exciting and working with it. That's what I ignited: American sportswear.

—*Ralph Lauren in* Ralph Lauren: The Man Behind the Mystique
by Jeffrey A. Trachtenberg

Lauren changed direction completely with his next women's wear collection. This time, he went back to the Victorian era for a soft, romantic look. Models featured high-necked blouses trimmed with lace and long skirts. Once again, the American public responded positively, and the collection was another huge, trendsetting style hit.

FROM FASHION TO FURNISHINGS

Lauren had been designing clothes for more than 10 years. By the early 1980s, he was ready to design something completely different. Much to the surprise of his admirers, Lauren announced he would be extending his brand to home furnishings. Lauren saw home furnishings as a natural extension of his lifestyle brands of clothing and fragrances.

Many people thought Lauren's idea was a bad one, but Lauren's friend and coworker Buffy Birrittella explained, "Ralph was the first designer to take his whole design concept from apparel into a full-blown home collection. Remember, we didn't just do tablewear or sheets or bathwear, we also did lifestyles within those categories."

In September 1983, he introduced the Ralph Lauren Home Collection. It was the first time a major clothing designer had moved into home furnishings. Much of the line would be manufactured by the J.P. Stevens Company, which was already well known as a maker of sheets and towels. J.P. Stevens manufactured sheets, pillowcases, comforters, and towels designed by Lauren. Other companies made glassware, china, silverware, and wall coverings. As always, Lauren thought big. He launched the entire line of 2,500 pieces at the same time.

Launching such a huge line all at once turned out to be a mistake. Soon the Home Collection was experiencing the same problems Polo and other Lauren divisions had: late deliveries, faulty merchandise, and no stock on the shelves when the stores needed it. Lauren's business partner, Peter Strom, summed up the situation when he said, "The interest was phenomenal. . . . But the marketing was disastrous, the merchandising needed a lot of help, and the production was terrible."

Lauren did not waste any time solving the problems. He saw that things were not working right and immediately made changes. In 1984, Lauren took control of production away from J.P. Stevens and two years later made it a division of his own Polo Ralph Lauren company. In 1986, the collection was relaunched and expanded to include furniture. This time, production and marketing worked well, and in just one year, the line was a big success. By 1988, Ralph Lauren Home Furnishings was doing almost $50 million a year in business selling an image that customers really wanted. As Jeffrey Trachtenberg explained, "Ralph didn't set out to peddle sheets and towels. The customers already had sheets and towels. Instead of selling cottons and flannels and terry cloth, Ralph sold the fantasy of how enjoyable it would be to share the same high-quality sheets and towels used in the best American and English homes."

Lauren divided his Home Collection into four distinct styles. New England featured traditional American styles. Log Cabin promoted Western styles and a rugged, outdoorsy image. Jamaica included relaxed tropical styles, and Thoroughbred focused on English heritage and culture with items that seemed to be from a classic English manor. Each style included furniture, sheets, towels, wall hangings, glassware, silverware, and more to bring the whole look together. For the first time, shoppers could find everything in one place to create an image in their own home.

Lauren extended his idea of creating a special world featuring his lifestyle to his advertisements. At first, his ads were only single pages in magazines, but later he hired fashion photographers to create ads that ran for 10 or 20 pages in the top magazines and newspapers. These advertisements featured elaborate sets and lighting and were a lot like movie sets. Lauren used models in his advertisements, but he frequently served as the model himself. "I appear occasionally in my ads," he told an interviewer. "Sometimes you want to say hello." Lauren also enjoyed being recognized in public. "When I walk down the street, people come up to me and say, 'I love your clothes,' or 'why don't you make this,' or 'your buttons fell off.'"

A STORE OF HIS OWN

The year 1986 saw Ralph Lauren moving into new territory in a different way. He had been one of the first designers to have his products located together in boutiques inside major department stores. Now he took the idea one step further and created an entire store dedicated to his clothes and home furnishings. The Polo Ralph Lauren store opened in the historic Rhinelander Mansion on Madison Avenue and Seventy-second Street in New York City. Before opening the store, Lauren renovated the mansion, which had originally been built in 1894 in the style of a French castle. It was one of the few times he poured a large amount of his own money into a project. The project took two years and about $30 million to finish.

Lauren's financial advisers told him that renovating the building and opening a store there was a bad idea. Lauren also faced negative comments from marketing and sales executives. People thought having a self-contained store would take business away from all the other locations that sold Lauren's products. Others did not like the location. As he had in the past, Lauren refused to listen to the criticism and remained true to his own idea.

Lauren's intuition paid off. As soon as the store opened, it became clear that its shoppers would have an experience like no other. The interior of the Rhinelander was set up like an English country estate, with beautiful details. The rooms were filled with props, and, of course, with Lauren's furniture, home furnishings, and clothes. Author Marvin Traub described the look: "Every detail was

Lauren's efforts to have his clothes placed in special sections of boutiques and department stores helped build his company's reputation. He was one of the first designers to go a step further when he opened his own brick-and-mortar operation to sell home furnishings in addition to clothes.

perfectly executed. Vintage tennis rackets and lacrosse sticks rested in rooms as if they'd just been left there a moment ago. When a book was on a shelf, it was a book, not a fake binding. It was as if the images in Lauren's head had finally become three-dimensional."

People flocked to the store to see his themed rooms and fashion collections and feel like they were a part of Lauren's upper-class world. In 1987, an article in *Women's Wear Daily* called the Rhinelander one of the top tourist attractions in New York City and reported the store had done more than $30 million in business during its first year. In addition, the Rhinelander increased traffic at other stores that sold Lauren's merchandise. The store's amazing success changed the face of retailing, as other designers began opening their own shops on a large scale.

A DARK SECRET

In 1986, Lauren was inducted into the Coty Hall of Fame. In September of that year, he appeared on the cover of *Time* magazine. No one looking at the designer's smiling face could have guessed that he was facing a serious personal crisis. Although he was at the peak of his success, Lauren had plenty to worry about. His father was very sick, and his brother Jerry had suffered a stroke a few months earlier. On top of all that, Lauren himself had a brain tumor. The tumor was not cancerous and was growing very slowly, but Lauren knew he faced a serious operation to remove it. Lauren had had the tumor for many years, but recently doctors advised him that it had become much bigger and had to be removed. When Lauren heard he needed surgery, he said, "That was about the scariest moment of my life."

Lauren kept his illness a secret from everyone except his family and closest friends. He said, "When I was on the cover of *Time*, and everybody thought I was riding high and the king, I knew I had to go in for the operation. I was living through my worst moments. No one has it all." He finished his fall 1987 collection before he went into the hospital. Finally, on April 13, 1987, Lauren underwent a five-and-a-half-hour surgery to remove the tumor. The surgery was a success, and Lauren left the hospital a week later. He spent the next four months recovering at several of his vacation homes. Rumors swirled through the industry that Lauren was dying. After a few months of recovery, Lauren made a few public appearances at fashion industry events and parties, and the rumors died down.

Finally, in August of 1987, Lauren returned to work. He had learned not to take anything for granted. "People have a tendency to forget about the good moments and what they have and what is so precious. It made me appreciate the things that are passing, that go too quickly, the moments when later you think, 'I could have done,' or 'I should have done.' That's how it affected me." Lauren was ready to take on the world again.

9

Beyond
the Business

Lauren's business continued to expand and prosper during the 1990s and the next decade. After the success of his store in the Rhinelander Mansion in New York City, Lauren opened more flagship stores around the world, including the largest Ralph Lauren store in the world, which opened in Tokyo in 2006. He also expanded his business into new ventures.

NEW INFLUENCES

Fashion had changed tremendously by the 1990s. Consumers no longer relied only on fashion designers to tell them what they should wear. Instead, people got ideas from rock-and-roll and hip-hop cultures or from styles seen on the street. Everyday dress also became more casual. Even office workers stopped dressing in suits and started going to work in khaki pants and nice shirts instead.

Lauren knew he had to change with the times, yet he still wanted to remain true to his classic look. He realized that young people wanted clothing that was edgier and reasonably priced. They also were very interested in athletics and being healthy and fit. To appeal to this market, Lauren created his Polo Sport line of athletic clothes. Lauren told the *New York Times*, "The fashion of the nineties is about health. And when I say health, I don't mean doctors. I mean body consciousness, consciousness of eating the right foods, throwing away the junk foods, feeling good on the inside and looking it on the outside."

Lauren also licensed a line of inexpensive jeans called Polo Jeans Company. The company's president, Mindy Grossman, made Lauren understand that he had to welcome new ideas if he wanted to appeal to young, modern shoppers. Polo Jeans Company was a good way to find new buyers and make them Polo customers for the rest of their lives. The new company was a success, making more than $100 million in its first year.

The year 1997 saw another milestone when Lauren took his company public. On June 11, Polo Ralph Lauren became a publicly traded company on the New York Stock Exchange. While Lauren still owned most of the company and had full control, now anyone could buy shares of stock, or ownership, in his company. The public offering raised enough money for Lauren to buy back some of the licenses he had sold to other companies and expand his business even further.

FAMILY TIES

Although he is extremely focused on his business, Lauren is very close to his family. He cared for his parents and grieved hard when they passed away within a few months of each other in 1994. Lauren has been married to Ricky for more than 45 years, and their children, now grown, are all successful, well-adjusted, and close to their parents and each other. Oldest son Andrew is a filmmaker who runs his own production company in New York City. Lauren's second son, David, began working for Polo Ralph Lauren in 2001 and went on to manage the company's global advertising and marketing campaigns. David was also responsible for the company's Rugby line of preppy fashions in 2004.

Daughter Dylan has gone into the business world in a different way. She is the owner of Dylan's Candy Bar, an upscale candy store with locations in New York and several other American cities. Dylan commented on the connection she has found between candy and fashion. "I think, growing up, the colors of my dad's collection of the polo shirts, and the cable knit sweaters . . . to me seemed like candy because they had these color swatches in a candy jar to choose from. It seemed edible. . . . I think the color sensitivity that I got was from that."

Dylan also shared the advice she received from her father. "He definitely said 'Do what you love and keep doing it, and enjoy what you're doing because this is your passion.' Stick to your guns basically, to your vision and your gut, which is very important." She also notes that she received a valuable education "just being around him and learning from him just by dinner conversations

Lauren's Vintage Automobiles

Lauren's wealth has allowed him to indulge in one of his favorite activities: collecting vintage cars. His personal automobile collection includes such treasures as a 1937 Alfa Romeo, a 1929 Bentley race car, a 1955 Mercedes 300SL Gull Wing Coupe, a 1965 Aston Martin DB5 Volante, and several Porsches, Jaguars, and Ferraris. In 2004, Lauren lent 16 of his cars to the Boston Museum of Fine Arts for a display called "Speed, Style, and Beauty."

or seeing how people react to him. . . . I think my dad's been very supportive of starting your own thing."

CHARITY, LAUREN STYLE

Lauren has also shared his huge personal fortune with others. He has hosted or appeared at many charitable events over the years, and he has also started his own charitable endeavors. He and Ricky established the Ralph Lauren Center for Cancer Care and Prevention at North General Hospital in Harlem, New York City, in 2000. His Polo Ralph Lauren Foundation also set up the American Heroes Fund after the devastating terror attacks of September

The Lauren family *(left to right, Andrew, Dylan, Ralph, Ricky, and David)* has found success in many ways. Apart from Ralph's achievements in fashion, Andrew, Dylan, and David have branched out into business and film.

After more than three decades at the top of the fashion industry, Lauren continues to create more of the classic clothes that have come to define American fashion. His empire has grown to include a dozen lines, spanning from men's eveningwear to skiwear.

11, 2001. The American Heroes Fund donated to various victims' charities and also set up scholarships for children of those killed in the attacks. Lauren also demonstrated his love for the performing arts when he and Ricky launched the Ralph and Ricky Lauren Center for the Performing Arts at New York's Lexington School for the Deaf.

Lauren has also given generously to the nation that he calls home. In 1998, this son of Russian immigrants donated $13 million to the Smithsonian Institution's National Museum of History to preserve the flag that inspired "The Star-Spangled Banner." When he made the donation, Lauren stated how proud he was to be an American. "The flag is an inspiration for all Americans and it

ELEMENTS OF STYLE

The key to longevity is to keep doing what you do better than anyone else. We work real hard at that. It's about getting our message out to the consumer. It's about getting their trust, but also getting them excited, again and again.

—*Ralph Lauren Hard Work Quotes*

captures the dreams and imaginations of men and women all over the world. I am a product of the American dream and the flag is its symbol."

Lauren is indeed an American success story. He started as the child of working-class immigrants and became one of the richest entrepreneurs in the world. Ralph Lauren is a man who changed the course of fashion and started a revolution that still influences how we dress today.

Chronology

1939	Ralph Lifshitz is born in the Bronx, New York.
1955	Changes last name to Lauren.
1968	Starts his own company, Polo.
1970	Wins his first Coty Award for best menswear design.
1972	Introduces his first women's wear collection.
1973	Polo Fashions comes close to bankruptcy; Lauren licenses his women's wear and Chaps lines to raise cash.

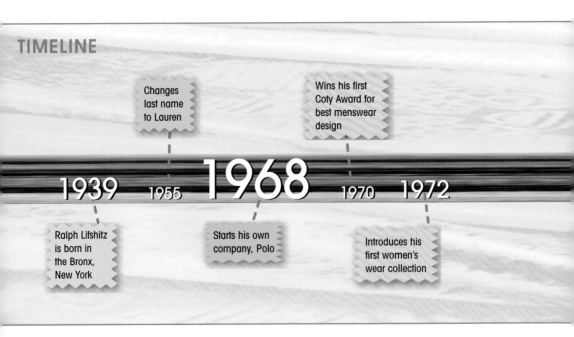

TIMELINE

Changes last name to Lauren

Wins his first Coty Award for best menswear design

1939 1955 1968 1970 1972

Ralph Lifshitz is born in the Bronx, New York

Starts his own company, Polo

Introduces his first women's wear collection

1976	Signs a deal to design fragrances.
1983	Introduces the Ralph Lauren Home Collection.
1986	The Polo Ralph Lauren store opens in New York City.
1987	Undergoes surgery to remove a brain tumor.
1997	Polo Ralph Lauren goes public and begins selling stock.
2005	Lauren's Automobile collection is displayed at Boston's Museum of Fine Arts.
2010	Decorated Chevalier de la Légion d'honneur by French president Nicolas Sarkozy.

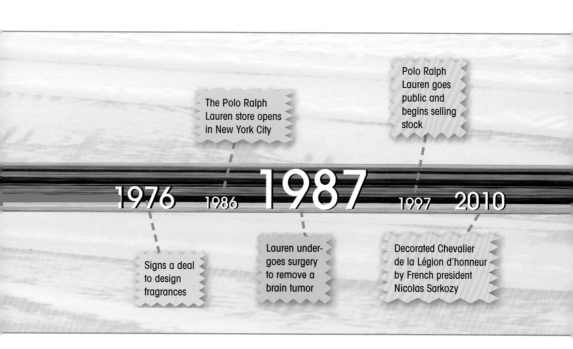

Glossary

accounts receivables   Money owed to a company for goods or services.

bankruptcy   A legal declaration that a company cannot pay its debts.

boutique   A small specialty shop.

chamois   A soft leather fabric.

conservative   Traditional.

entrepreneur   A person who starts and runs his or her own business.

exclusive   Something only available in a few places.

fit model   A model who works with pattern makers to determine the proper fit of a garment.

flagship   The largest or most important branch of a store or business.

fragrances   Perfumes or colognes.

inventory   A list of goods a business has on hand.

line   A single type of merchandise that includes different styles and sizes.

logo   A name or symbol that identifies a product or company name.

marketing   Advertising strategies used to encourage people to buy a product or service.

merchandise   Goods that are bought and sold.

petite Small.

preppy A style of dress characterized by classic clothing worn by prep-school students.

remnants Bits of material left over from making clothes.

retailers Stores that sell goods to the public.

Bibliography

BOOKS

Gross, Michael. *Genuine Authentic: The Real Life of Ralph Lauren*. New York: HarperCollins, 2003.

McDowell, Colin. *Ralph Lauren: The Man, the Vision, the Style*. London: Octopus Publishing Group Limited, 2002.

Milbank, Caroline Reynolds. *New York Fashion: The Evolution of American Style*. New York: Harry N. Abrams, Inc., 1989.

Trachtenberg, Jeffrey A. *Ralph Lauren: The Man Behind the Mystique*. Boston: Little, Brown and Company, 1988.

Traub, Marvin. *Like No Other Store: The Bloomingdale Legend*. New York: Random House, 1993.

MAGAZINE ARTICLE

Winfrey, Oprah. "Oprah Talks to Ralph Lauren." *O, The Oprah Winfrey Magazine*, October 2002.

WEB SITES

Bloomingdale's—Our History
http://www1.bloomingdales.com/media/about/history.jsp
Retrieved July 2, 2010.

Coco Chanel Biography
http://www.biography.com/articles/Coco-Chanel-9244165
Retrieved August 7, 2010.

"The History of Neckties: A Visual Timeline of the Tie's History"
http://www.abcneckties.com/necktiehistory.html
Retrieved August 1, 2010.

Kugel, Allison. "Dylan Lauren: Daughter of Fashion Designer Ralph Lauren Makes Her Own Sweet Dreams a Reality with Dylan's Candy Bar"
http://www.pr.com/article/1041
Retrieved August 1, 2010.

Official Ralph Lauren Web Site
http://about.polo.com
Retrieved June 30, 2010.

Ralph Lauren Biography
http://www.woopidoo.com/biography/ralph-lauren/index.htm
Retrieved June 30, 2010.

Ralph Lauren—Lauren's Childhood Acting Dream
http://www.contactmusic.com/news.nsf/story
laurens-childhood-acting-dream_1036754
Retrieved June 30, 2010.

WIC—Women's History in America
http://www.wic.org/misc/history.htm
Retrieved August 1, 2010.

Further Resources

BOOKS

Bolino, Monica, ed. *Fashion*. San Diego, Calif.: Greenhaven Press, 2002.

Weatherly, Myra. *Business Leaders: Ralph Lauren*. Greensboro, N.C.: Morgan Reynolds Publishing Company, 2009.

WEB SITES

Ralph Lauren Biography

http://www.notablebiographies.com/Ki-Lo/Lauren-Ralph.html

"Ralph Lauren." Biography Resource Center. Farmington Hills, Mich.: Gale, 2010.

http://galenet.galegroup.com/servlet/BioRC

Picture Credits

Index

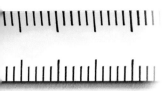

About the Author

JOANNE MATTERN has written more than 300 books for children and teens. She specializes in nonfiction and especially enjoys writing about animals and nature, sports, history, and biographies. *Ralph Lauren* is her third biography for Chelsea House; she has also written Chelsea House biographies of Eva Peron and William Penn. Mattern lives in New York State with her husband, four children, and a menagerie of pets.